THE
FREE CHURCH
AND
SEDUCTIVE
CULTURE

By Calvin Redekop

Diagrams by Ivan Moon

 HERALD PRESS, SCOTTDALE, PENNSYLVANIA

PREFACE

"The true believers show in act and deed that they believe, are born of God and spiritually minded. They lead a pious, unblamable life before all men, they break the bread of peace with their beloved brethren, as a proof and testimony that they are one with Christ and His church. . . . They walk in love and mercy, they serve their neighbors. . . . In short, they order their lives, in their weaknesses, according to all the words, commandments, ordinances, spirit, rule, example, and measure of Christ, as the Scriptures teach; for they are in Christ and Christ is in them."

This statement might easily be dismissed as one more contemporary pious oration thrown into the harsh face of hate, deceit, war, and evil. There is a difference, for this statement, penned some four hundred and twenty-five years ago, presaged a tradition that has tried to take its contents seriously. The present author, a member of this tradition, is inextricably caught in the web of human action and institutions that have emerged as the result of the attempt to become "true believers." The agony and ecstasy of the failures and achievements of the goal has put a peculiar stamp on members of this tradition. It has created an ambivalence in the hearts of many adherents borne out of despair.

It is the assumption, however, of this volume that the principles that have animated the adherents of the "free church vision" are destined to become the principles of increasing numbers of Christians as they become aware of the process by which they have been seduced by their environment. The question is whether the Christian church will be freed from its seduction soon enough to make a difference in God's plan. That Christians will come to the conclusion, for example, that war and killing in any form is totally contrary to the will of God is a matter of time — before or after the holocaust?

The first chapter points out some of the ways in which religion (Christianity, the focus in this book) will need to respond and change if it is to be meaningful for its adherents. The

3

second chapter presents an analysis of how some of the leading social scientists look at religion, and what relevancy they see in religion for the solving of some of society's major ills. The third chapter describes some of the factors which have contributed to the seduction of the Christian church to secular culture, using the Crusades as a case study. Chapters four and five deal with the attempts by some of the harassed "sectarian" Christian groups to achieve a church free of "ideology" or the seduction of the transcendental religion into a prostituted one. The early Anabaptist origins are analyzed for the insights they offer concerning the protest of total ideology. Chapter six is the "Achilles Heel" of the thesis, in which a case study of the Old Colony Mennonites reveals the precariousness of the free church vision. The final two chapters attempt to analyze the structures which contribute to confrontation of vital issues to assure that the unseduced free church may emerge and prosper.

The message of this book has been mentally written and re-written several times. The inspiration to put the message in this form came as the result of an invitation to present the term address at Tabor College's (Kansas) first interterm in 1968, entitled "Christian Responsibility in a World of Change," later published in *The Journal of Church and Society* (Spring, 1968). Tabor's warm reception of the address provided the motivation to recast the material in its present form.

Special thanks is given to Goshen College which, through a faculty research committee, provided some needed financial support for secretarial help and research facilities. The greatest thanks, however, is given to the hundreds of students that I have been privileged to lead in a common search at Hesston College, Tabor College, Earlham College, Earlham School of Religion, Goshen College, and the Associated Mennonite Biblical Seminaries. They have contributed immeasurably to my growth and illustrate the biblical and sociological truth that "all of us . . . form one body" (Romans 12:5). It is to this generation of students that this book is dedicated.

Calvin Redekop
Goshen College

INTRODUCTION

Three perspectives on America's religious experience have emerged during recent decades. A brief review of these perspectives furnishes a backdrop against which we can appreciate Calvin Redekop's proposal in this text.

H. Richard Niebuhr developed what can be called a confessional perspective in his volume, *The Kingdom of God in America*. He traced the vitality of American religion to a transcendent ideal of the kingdom of God. He followed out the various forms in which that ideal found expression and underwent degradation. The confessional heritage was thus understood as the source and renewing power of the public welfare — transforming public good in its moments of authenticity and losing itself in worldliness in moments of debasement.

Sidney Mead developed a rather different perspective over these decades. He interprets America's religious experience in two broad streams of vitality — a religion of the churches and a religion of democracy. The religion of the churches has been a particularistic, confessional strand with a variety of denominational expressions. After the separation of church and state, this pluriform confessional strand shared in the religion of democracy but clung to its particular creedal and ritual traditions. The religion of democracy drew from the enlightenment tradition and found primary expression in the legal order of American life. Thus the common elements of American religion — trust in deity, an assurance of reward and punishment, and a moral order of freedom, equality, and justice — found embodiment in a common faith of public life. Confessional faith was understood to contribute to public welfare through cultivation of moral character and support of public good; so the ambiguity in the relationship of these two religious strands could be lived through in a tolerable tension.

A third, less prominent, perspective has been articulated in recent years by Robert Bellah. In his essay, "Civil Religion in America," he developed the symbolism, rituals, and communal order in the public strand of American religion which Sidney

5

Mead calls the religion of democracy. This third perspective, finding the mainstream of religious vitality in the civil religion, has been an implicit strand of thought in much social scientific literature, though it has seldom found explicit formulation. Perhaps the most thoroughgoing statement was made some years back by W. Lloyd Warner in his study of symbols in Yankee City, *The Living and the Dead*. However, Warner's study investigated both confessional and civil strands, whereas Robert Bellah's evolutionary notion of a gradual secularization of religion leads him to focus on civil religion somewhat to the neglect of the confessional strand. If one assumes that the West is going through a gradual secularization of religious symbols, then one is inclined to look for the central stream of religious vitality outside the traditional stream of confessional churches. And this is precisely the orientation which guides Robert Bellah's attention to the public or civil religion.

At the risk of covering over many interpretations of religion in America, we settle tentatively then for three broad perspectives. One view can be called confessional because it traces the founding, empowering, and renewing of American life to the confessional heritages of the various denominations, looking to the churches to strengthen and reform the public life of America. Another view can be called the two communities, because it sees two interwoven but separable communities and covenants at the source of American life and flowing together through America's anguished and turbulent development. The revelatory covenant of confessional faith is thus intertwined with the natural covenant of human rights, coming to expression in many denominational communities or voluntary associations in the private sphere and a limited state under Constitution in the public sphere. And thirdly the civil view which locates the mainstream of religious and moral vitality in the public or societal faith as it found expression in the Declaration of Independence, the Constitution, statements of leaders and public figures, a revolutionary deliverance and profound suffering in civil strife, culminating in the contemporary struggle to come to terms with its power and world position.

Calvin Redekop develops a free church vision in line with the confessional perspective. He finds the degradation of religious vitality in conformity to the interests and struggle for power in the public world; so civil religion for Mr. Redekop tends to be a debased religiousness. This is not to say that he agrees fully with H. R. Niebuhr's interpretation of America's religious experience. Mr. Redekop stands within the tradition of what George Williams called "The Radical Reformation." He is proffering the Anabaptist vision of a vital, pure, culturally and ideologically free life in faith. He sees the center of this faith in communal life as it grounds itself in the scriptural word and seeks a disciplined life together. Whereas H. R. Niebuhr took a more and more sanguine view of religious institutions in his later writings, even talking about ministers in organizational terms as "pastoral directors," Calvin Redekop sees the demonic debasement of religious vitality in cultural and institutional forms. Consequently we have here a clear and cogently argued case for a radical, confessional expression of religious vitality in American life — looking to constant revolutionary openness to the leading of the Spirit in the community as the real dynamic of authentic religiousness and public responsibility.

This radical tradition has a significant and honored place in American religious history. Sectarian communities, evangelical revivals, spiritual fellowships, communities of discipline, and vital religious fellowships have constantly nurtured America's religious life. Many of our denominations are later organizational expressions of such religious movements. Indeed a whole sociology of transition from sect to denomination has developed in the study of America's religious life. But this is not for a moment to suggest that the argument of this text is just one more case being made for radical confessionalism. Even if one holds with the notion of two religious communities or leans to the civil religion interpretation, there is a serious question whether America any longer has religious resources to limit and restrain her surfeit of power. Now the militarizing of her foreign policy and the escalation of police suppression in her urban areas make her civil religion into little more than a

7

justification for an "Arrogance of Power." And the bureaucratization of public life in what is now called the military-
industrial-governmental complex makes the political leader less
accessible to public criticism. And in turn this invisible government creates deeper and deeper frustrations in the young,
leading them to excesses in their attempts to gain a hearing
or create a public forum. So the free church vision has its own
seasonal relevance in our time. The denominations are themselves so entangled in bureaucratic organization and large-
scale financing that they are retreating from the prophetic
task; in fact, they are already experiencing radical polarization
within their memberships as a consequence of the past decade
of public witness. If there is to be challenge to this arrogant
expression of power in our public life, it may only come from
such committed, unencumbered, and disciplined communal fellowships. This is the case that Mr. Redekop makes, and in doing
so he can draw upon many years of careful study of the
strengths and weaknesses of this free church tradition.

I hold one reservation about Calvin Redekop's proposal which
should be mentioned to keep the record straight. My reservation is grounded in a view that religious vitality and cultural
forms are always inextricably intertwined. And indeed I concur
with Sidney Mead's view of America's religious experience,
though I trace out the significance of this experiment and
its implications for the confessional heritage somewhat differently.
But my principal concern here is with the profound religious
struggle in the new generation. The whole style of this struggle
is offensive to the denominational and free church traditions.
The concern for personal sensibility, human intimacy, communal
freedom, and mind-expanding experiences is alien to our religious cultures. Yet the deepest religious strivings seem to be
finding expression in these various movements among the
youth. And it appears that religious renewal and a restraint
on American power can only come as these new religious
vitalities are tapped. But what criteria can the free church
vision employ to discriminate the authentic from the inauthen-
tic in this new religious movement? Or does this radical con-

fessionalism discount all of these vitalities and look for a religion beyond religions, a spiritual culture beyond cultures? Is culture, then, the real embarrassment to the free church vision or only the rigidity, moralism, and irrelevance of our cultural styles? If the latter, then perhaps the new movements among the young may be the most fertile ground for this free church vision.

Gibson Winter

December 1969
The Divinity School
University of Chicago

TABLE OF CONTENTS

LIST OF FIGURES AND TABLES

An Overview of the Role of Religion in Society

"Thus, in starkest form, the question about the evolutionary fate of religion is a question about the fate of supernaturalism. To the question put in this way, the answer must be that the evolutionary future of religion is extinction. Belief in supernatural beings and in supernatural forces that affect nature without obeying nature's laws will erode and become only an interesting historical memory."[1]

This orientation toward religion expressed by Anthony Wallace is probably typical of most members of contemporary western society. Many "modern" people see religion as some type of "hang over." They regard it as an illusion, a vestige of the past, an opiate of the masses, a stage in the evolution of society, prelogical thinking, or a projection of unknown fears.

In spite of intermittent flurries of excitement that accompany rumors of the revivals of religion, whether they are eastern or western; in spite of reports of record amounts of construction of religious edifices; and in spite of reports of increases in membership of this cult or that sect, religion is still believed to be undergoing a decline in its power to influence men. Because of the advance of science and technology, it is alleged, world religions of almost every variety have been forced to retreat and find a cave where they can, unmolested, concern themselves with "metaphysics and morality."[2]

However, there remains a recurring, nagging doubt that religion can really be dispensed with that easily. For to some observers religion is not dead, nor does it appear to be dying. One sociologist, Kingsley Davis, believes that religion is not so easily done away with, since many problems are involved in simply understanding its functions, let alone stating categorically whether it is declining or not. Further, Davis doubts that religion will die because it has an uncanny ability to adapt itself; that it "changes along with the rest of society."[3]

Beyond this the problem of definition is so great that no consensus exists as to what religion really is. One expert refuses to make a definitive statement about the essence of religion — "Let me reaffirm, first of all, my skepticism as to the adequacy of any definition purporting to summarize the totality of phenomena labeled 'religion.' "[4] Thus it is a moot point to say that religion is declining or increasing in influence. If in addition we note the confusion resulting from religion adapting itself to society, it becomes still more difficult to declare whether or not religion is in trouble.

Therefore if there is no agreement about what is being discussed, if there is a very intimate and confused relationship between what each of us and the rest of society are talking about, there really may not be much meaningful left to say! Nevertheless, most people have some general idea of what they mean when they talk about religion, and this will be enough to get the discussion started. In the process a "working definition" will emerge as the argument develops.

With this proviso, it may be possible to use the broadest description of religion — institutional membership — as an indication of the shape of world religion. The following table indicates what appears to be a reasonable description of the situation regarding religious institutional membership:

Table 1

Estimated Membership of Principal Religions of the World (1967)°

Religion	World	% of Total
Christian	977,383,000	28.82
Roman Catholic	(600,768,000)	17.71
Eastern Orthodox	(146,080,000)	4.30
Protestant	(230,535,000)	6.79
Jewish	13,537,000	.39
Muslim	474,309,000	13.98
Zoroastrian	150,000	.04
Shinto	70,363,000	2.07
Taoist	54,324,000	1.60
Confucian	371,587,000	10.95
Buddhist	171,764,000	5.06
Hindu	424,397,000	12.51
Others and none	834,058,000	24.59

Total World Population   3,391,854,000

°Source: "Religion," *Britannica Book of the Year* (Chicago: *Encyclopedia Britannica*, 1968), p. 669.

13

According to the small percentage of "others and none," religious adherence follows rather carefully the profile masses of populations of the world. The proportion of those considered to have no religious affiliation amounts to about 24.6 percent of total world population. Ten years ago the "others and none" figure represented 15.7 percent of total population, which suggests a considerable drop in religious membership. However, the 1967 category of "others and none" included primitive religions, which was not included in the earlier estimate.

These figures should not be considered any criterion for the role of religion in the world today. They merely suggest that religion is still a formidable factor, even when one uses the figures provided by religious institutions about their own strength. The subjective ("intrinsic" to Allport) aspects of religion, the significance of the religion for the behavior of the individual, and the institutional commitment of the religious adherents can only be speculated about and are not susceptible to analysis at this point in social science research.

In light of how difficult it is to describe objectively the relative strength or weakness of world religion, it is surprising that religion is receiving increasing support from social scientists of late. Whereas social scientists earlier assumed that religion was probably doomed, more and more sociologists and anthropologists today are regarding religion as seriously as they do other aspects of the social structure. Thus Lowie says:

> I cannot say that I have become a religious man as a result of my study, but I have become an informed one; and I have seen too much to believe now in the dicta that I accepted in my youth. I no longer doubt that religion has a definite place in human life.[5]

Kingsley Davis, cited above, offers an even more outspoken defense of religion: "So universal, permanent, and pervasive is religion in human society that unless we understand it thoroughly we shall fail to understand society."[6]

A defense of the viability of religion is raised in at least two ways. The first is indicated by Lowie, who uses the taxonomical approach. That is, he defines religion in a certain way (for example, as psychological devotion) and then proceeds to suggest the law that since man will always invest some objects with psychological devotion, religion will always remain. The second is indicated by the functionalist point of view, which suggests that certain things must be achieved in a society for that society to survive. Since religion is indispensable in meeting some of these needs, it will survive. As Davis says, "One of the functions of religion is to justify, rationalize, and support the sentiments that give cohesion to society."[7] An important qualification by most functionalists, however, is that if another institution were to emerge which would provide the functions that religion serves, then religion might well disappear.

That this view of religion (i.e., its importance in human life) is a serious one, is evidenced and supported by religion's gaining strength as a subject of study in anthropology and sociology; by the amount of research in religion that is being supported and reported; and by the way religion departments are springing up on many university campuses in the United States and abroad. Religion is coming into its own among scholars and intellectuals. But the man in the pew is ostensibly not interested, as is evidenced in research which indicates the looseness with which lower classes, especially in the West, respond to religion.

It appears that the religions of the world are the objects of some respect and support by outsiders — including academicians — but the object of some ridicule and disinterest by insiders. The criticism of religion from within, however, is nothing new. Very few religions have not had "palace revolts" and internal dissension, protest movements, schisms, and general disaffection. In fact, it can probably be proved that the more healthy a religion is, the more inner ferment, disagreement, and chaos there is.

The history of Judaism bears this proposition out. The thundering prophets had little good to say about the Judaism of their own time. In some cases they were not only the mouthpieces of God's word, but secretly, and sometimes not so secretly, wished the destruction of the religious society. Jesus Himself was rather critical of Judaism, and was finally crucified for His stringent demands for reform. The same can be said for most other religions. Joachim Wach states, "All world religions face periodic protests against the main trend of their development. These occur in three fields of religious expression — in theology, in cult, in organization." [8]

Christianity is not the least among religions if the amount of protest and criticism is the criterion for judging. Christianity has experienced multitudes of protesters: saints such as Saint Francis; defiant reformers such as Martin Luther; sarcastic surgeons such as Erasmus; and a most impressive array of schismatic groups which have protested and criticized the conditions that obtained in normal church life. Some of the most eloquent and erudite literature available to man is the result of protest to religion, e.g., Soren Kierkegaard's criticism of Protestant Christianity.

Religion appears, therefore, to be secure — at least for the moment. It is being defended by social scientists. Its health is further attested to by internal dissent and criticism. Both counts, however, leave religion in a vulnerable position, for social scientists are suggesting that religion is useful only as long as it performs certain functions better than other developing forms. At the same time the inner protests against religion are reaching such proportions that reform will need to come soon if both the inner members of religion and its external defenders are to remain sympathetic to religion.

The description of the world which the Christian religion confronts depends upon the frame of reference from which the conditions are viewed. This need for a reference point is best indicated by a man who asked a friend, "And how is your wife?" to which the friend replied, "As compared to what?" The world can be described from various points of view, but in this discussion the perspective will be that of the person who sees the world from a deep commitment to the goals of the Christian gospel. The conditions that will be analyzed will therefore be conditions which are significant for the survival of society from a sociological-scientific point of view, and significant for

16

full realization of integrity and meaning of human existence from a Christian point of view.

Take the problem of war. The use of warfare to solve social and political problems is one of the major and increasingly crucial problems of modern society. Warfare has a long and tenacious history, though there are societies on record which did not depend upon war to solve problems.[9] The environment of Christianity's conception and nurture has been infested with warfare and conflict. The Rome of early Christianity was based on a military empire extended by conquest. The emergence and development of the nations of Europe, which became the strongholds of Christianity, involved incessant warfare. The American revolution, often proudly hailed as a war to free religion from authoritarian domination, nevertheless was a war.

The Christian church itself became involved in making war, often in the interests of extending the rule of God, as in the almost incredible Crusades beginning in 1096 and the conquests of Vladimir of Russia.[10] The wars following the Reformation were almost entirely internecine conflicts concerned with establishing boundaries of dominance, culminating in the now famous *cujus regio ejus religio* (the prince determines the religion in his land).[11] This fact has caused at least one pragmatist to say, "The great days of religions have been the days of hostility, between the religions, between the church and the sects, or between different churches."[12]

War continues to plague the Christian West. In fact, some authorities propose that the resort to war to solve international problems is increasing rather than decreasing. In the first seventy years of a century that was to be the "Christian century," western Christian nations have been involved in at least four major wars, and some realists are seriously suggesting that the final war is only a matter of time.

Statistics on war are not very meaningful, for they cannot convey its unfathomable misery and tragedy. Nevertheless, they do convey some perspective from which to gauge the scale and role of war. In the three major wars (World War I, World War II, and the Korean War) approximately 21 million military men lost their lives, and an estimated 24 million civilians lost their lives in direct or indirect relationship to these wars.[13] Some of the major national revolutions have added millions to the death toll. The carnage of wars of national liberation offers another tragic statistic, though these wars probably enlist more support and moral justification than all other types of wars. No estimates are available regarding the human cost in these wars, but the grim toll continues to mount.

War is one of the major human "traps" that face mankind.[14] It is a trap in at least three respects: first, the next war may provide for the final extermination of mankind; second, as the Vietnam war clearly demonstrates, war depraves the people who participate in it; and last, war creates more problems than it solves. These conclusions are now becoming clear to increasing numbers of the human family, but, tragically, they are apparently helpless to do anything about it.

War has been a part of the environment in which Christianity has lived. The relationship of the Christian church to war is complex, but the following are among the theoretical possibilities: (1) the Christian church has been the cause of many major conflicts involving war and bloodshed; (2) the Christian church has actively participated in many of the major conflicts, although it has not perpetrated them, (3) the Christian church has ignored and/or evaded participation in some conflicts or parts of conflicts; (4) the Christian church has actively opposed the pursuit of military and armed conflict.

In actual practice, Christians have participated in each of the categories to various degrees during various conflicts. The implications of war for the shape of Christianity cannot be expanded upon here. It can, however, be said unequivocally that Christ's gospel is a gospel of love, and that John states it clearly when he says, "He who does not love remains in death. Anyone who hates his brother is a murderer, and you know that no murderer has eternal life abiding in him."[15] The fate of Christianity is inextricably bound up in what it does about war. At present the successful solution to this problem is by no means assured for the Christian church.

Another environmental condition that has confronted Christianity throughout its history is the presence of rich and poor, the majority in the subordinated and exploited poor classes. The Old Testament prophets inveighed heavily against the people "who trample upon the poor."[16] Christ emphasized the importance of the gospel to the poor, and says He came to bring the gospel to the needy, rather than to the rich. Some of His most powerful teachings, including those of Lazarus and the simile of the camel and the eye of the needle, suggest a strong position regarding the poor.

Just what the nature and extent of poverty in the world was in which Christianity thrived is difficult to determine. During the birth of Christianity, Rome had such a large contingent of poor that a vast system of dole kept the poor alive. The threat of famine ever before most citizens of Europe brought about the development of military defenses against sudden attack by the poor demanding bread. The Peasants' War and the Muenster Rebellion are only a few of the more celebrated illustrations of the rebellion of the poor.

The plight of the poor has received great publicity in recent years as it has been shown that poverty can exist in the backyard of the wealthiest nation on earth. In 1962, an estimated 33 to 35 million Americans "were living at or below the boundaries of poverty. . . . "[17] This was almost a fifth of the nation's entire population. The nature and extent of poverty is much worse in Latin America.

The following factors make poverty in contemporary times very different from poverty in earlier times: (1) Technologically speaking, there is no longer any reason for the poor to exist, since productivity could supply enough for all. (2) In recent times, the acceptance of poverty as a way of life, or as ordained for a segment of the population, has been increasingly rejected, largely because of the effects of mass media and because of the technological potential for alleviating it.

Just as poverty has been looked at from various positions, so the Christian church has also taken various positions toward it. Christians have frequently glorified poverty and encouraged it. Thus the mendicant monks, and a wealthy church depending upon taxation from the peasants to maintain its life, preached and encouraged the life of poverty — one by faith, the other because it was "good business." Some of the more "Platonic" or spiritualistic Christian believers have also de-emphasized the value and importance of material goods. Other Christians have been less approving of poverty, but have nevertheless believed that material wealth tends to divert the believer from the real essence of Christianity, namely, the spiritual disciplines and eternal values. John Wesley comes to mind as an illustration of this position, although numerous others could be cited.

A more positive stance toward wealth is taken by Christians who believe that the creation, a large part of which is material, is for man's benefit and therefore to be utilized and enjoyed. The material world is therefore not to be shunned, but rather to be enjoyed as part of God's plan for His people. A final position is that God's salvation of His people will come almost entirely through the transformation of the objective and material world, by which each individual will receive his share of material wealth in order for him to achieve true personhood and meaning.

Although Christians throughout the centuries have taken these quite different stances regarding wealth, considerable evidence suggests that Christ took a clear and unequivocal position on material goods and wealth as it relates to the disparity between the rich and the poor. The causes for the church's failure to follow Christ's teaching on the subject must again be left for later analysis. It is sufficient here to cite only one or two of Christ's statements regarding the disciples' stance concerning poverty: "The Spirit of the Lord is upon me, because he has anointed me to preach good news to the poor."[18] "Come, O blessed of my Father, inherit the kingdom prepared for you from the foundation of the world; for I was hungry and you gave me food. . . ."[19]

Just as it cannot ignore war, the Christian church will realize its integrity and purpose only if it speaks meaningfully and significantly to poverty. It is not a foregone conclusion that it has done so or will do so in the near future.

Another environmental factor which has been of signal importance for religion in general and for Christianity in the West is what has been called "domination" or "superordination-subordination." Instances of this phenomenon existed before Moses, but the celebrated story of his attempts to get Pharaoh to "let my people go" describes well the practice of some people dominating others and anticipates the Negro struggle. Documentation of man's attempts to dominate others throughout history is scarcely necessary. In fact, most human history has been written from the perspective of military and political domination of one person or group over others.

Domination in human history well deserves the description of Giddings, Hobbes, and others, who see human history as the story of "red tooth and claw." But domination of one person or group over another is well illustrated by the history of the Armenian people. Armenian history reveals a people subjected successively by the Persians, the Saracens (Mohammedans), Mongolians, and Turks, to name only the most important of earlier conquerors of Armenia. Only one case, from the year 1049, can be cited. The Seljukian Turks, after having surrounded the city of Arzu, laid siege. "Of the one hundred and fifty thousand inhabitants and those who had taken refuge in the city, some were butchered in cold blood, some were roasted to death, and the rest carried into captivity."[20] The Armenian story parallels that of other groups, the most modern and recent example being the Jews in Germany (though by no means in Germany alone, for Russian and Eastern European countries have been aggressive in dominating Jews).

Domination, however, need not be considered only in its extreme form. The social and economic exploitation of individuals or groups against their own will (or even with their consent when brainwashing has been complete, as with some "Uncle Tom" Negroes in American history) is a domination possibly more pervasive and sweeping than the physical and political types de-

21

scribed above. Economic and/or racial domination — where one group is able to exploit and keep in subjection other individuals or groups — is possibly the most general type which does not require a Marxist or evolutionary orientation to uncover. Domination can also be individual, in which one person imposes his will over another, and includes the relationships of marriage partners, business partners, or professors and their students.

The stance of the Christian church toward domination may again be categorized. (1) The church has been dominant over an entire culture. The Medieval Church, beginning around the year 300 and ending around 1300, had as its objective the domination of an entire civilization. The "three great Latin church fathers, St. Jerome, St. Ambrose, and St. Augustine, writing at the end of the fourth and the beginning of the fifth century, gave to the church well-informed and judicious opinion on every aspect of Christian life and civilization."[21] This has been termed the period of *Corpus Christianum*, in which the entire culture was under the domination of the Christian church and its heads.

(2) The church has also been a dominant force over those who belong to the church or have committed themselves to the Holy Covenant. The best examples of this stance are Calvin's Geneva and the Puritan Church in New England. Both attempted to dominate their adherents in almost every aspect of life. In some dimensions their stance seems almost to parallel the church during the *Corpus Christianum*. Although it stopped short of controlling the entire culture, it did dominate the affairs of most social institutions, including the state, in certain ways at some historical points, such as occurred in early New England, where only members of privileged religious denominations could participate in the political affairs.

(3) The church has also enjoyed a position of domination, never consciously organized, but representing a "segmental" position, with various expressions. Here the church did not fully control the external social and political life, but did control other segments of the environment, such as the teaching of morality in public schools.

22

(4) Finally, the church has sought to dominate in a clearly limited sense and within a prescribed circle of persons. Such a domination was exercised by group decision or agreement ("consensus" or "brotherhood" were synonymous terms) and limited in its power or authority to those who have voluntarily committed themselves to the group in question. There was no attempt to dominate those who were not in the circle of society, since they were considered outside the legitimate rule of Christ. Strict rules of behavior were incumbent on the membership, and if there was noncompliance, excommunication from the group was the only recourse. The followers of Menno Simons with their strong emphasis on church discipline and excommunication are among the best illustrations of this position.[22]

This concept of human domination is both very complex and very central to human life. It is not possible to do more than allude to its importance and its role here. It is truly one of the great issues of human life, and one which the Christian church has dealt with, although often not to her credit. Some of the most sordid examples of human domination come from the life of the church itself. The missionary compound of classical missionary times is one of the more sophisticated, yet nevertheless real illustrations of this fact.

Nationalism, another factor present in every society, can take forms varying from arrogant ignorance of all other societies to aggressive nationalism. Orientals have for many years accused Occidentals of extreme ethnocentrism, as expressed in imperialistic aggression. Although the Oriental may be correct in his assessment, eastern religions have tended to make as many inroads in the West as Occidental religions have in the Orient.

The Christian church's position regarding nationalism has been checkered. The early church was the opposite of an ethnocentric movement. Its strong missionary zeal made it the most inclusive movement that the world has seen. During the so-called Dark Ages, the Christian church was developing an exclusive ethnocentric structure. This structure, however, did not express strong nationalistic flavor until it emerged during the

Crusades, in which many of the conflicts were really a mixture of religion and nationalism. The Christian church's support of the European occupation of Africa, its establishment of missionary outposts in China and other parts of the Orient, and its approval of the extermination of the Indian in the United States so that the church could fulfill its "destiny," illustrate Christianity's identification of state interests and imperialistic expansion with its own calling.

The Christian church has not been uniform, however, in its support of ethnocentrism: Some church groups have been anti-nationalist, without having evangelistic urges. The Armenians, for example, have rarely, if ever, imposed their will on anyone. More contemporary examples would be the Doukhobors and the Hutterites, who, although very much convinced of their religious views, have not imposed them on others or identified them with national objectives.

Some church groups have actively "proselyted" others into the groups' own systems without becoming involved in any coercion involving the state or nationalism. The Jehovah's Witnesses and Mormons illustrate this stance, as do the Mennonites and their strongly missionary forebears, the Anabaptists. All show strong outreach, but little if any identification with national aims and objectives.

For a long time the Christian church has found itself implicated with partial blending of national and church objectives and activities. The Constantine era, considered the downfall of the church, tended to align the objectives of the state and the church, so that what was good for the Christian church was good for the Roman Empire. In this kind of relationship, the church has identified with the state in many areas, including support of certain wars and other expansions if they seemed to the church to be beneficial for its own objectives. An illustration of this position is the Dutch Reformed Church in South Africa, which seems a direct offspring of the Anglican Church's relation to the English crown.

Finally, the church has also identified its own objectives with those of the nation. In this stance, the nation's goals and means of achieving them are also those of the church. Although the Christian church may never have taken this position as a body, individuals and groups within the church have taken this position, as some far right groups in America have demonstrated and as the "national" churches did in Germany during World War II.

Another aspect of the environment which has always concerned religious people in general and Christians in particular is secularism. This concept has been at the basis of much of the activity of the Christian church throughout its history, and has motivated many thinkers to build systems of culture. It has been variously defined, and the controversy now raging concerning its definition merely highlights the importance of this entity. For our purposes, secularism will be defined as the denial of a transcendental dimension to human experience, and the consequent refusal to be guided or directed by a transcendental authority or force. [23]

Anthropologically speaking, human society began as a sacred society. All of human life and activity was suffused with an awareness of, and submission to, an alleged external and supernatural being or force. But the supernatural went through various stages of development in the West, according to the anthropologists. It began with polytheism, moved through conflicting monotheisms to a very personal human-like God, then to a scientific God — a *Deus Ex Machina* — and now finally to a "dead God."

Secularism was an inexorable movement in the environment in which Christianity grew to maturity. The monotheism of Judaism had a difficult time, for it faced constant tendencies to go after other gods, or to forsake gods entirely and serve human gods, such as wealth or power. After Christianity had established its leadership in Western Europe, the temptation to secularism developed within the church itself, so that the emergence of monasticism served to save the church from complete secularism, which had been brought there by wealth and power.

But secularism was a great temptress, and what she failed to gain through the use of wealth, power, and domination, she obtained through the development of the intellect. The Enlightenment and the beginning of the scientific revolution brought secularism into the church in a way never known before. The Christian God became the "God of the Gaps," and leading writers could call Him "the gaseous vertebrate" or the "fat lady." The emancipated man began to see Christianity as one of "the fantastic products of human imbecility. . . . "[24]

From the perspective of the Christian, secularism has never been a value-free concept. It has always meant unfaithfulness to the message and life of Christ. Naturally enough, "secularism" has always been a term reserved for others — individuals, groups, or denominations which have held positions regarding the Christian way of life and differing from one's own. Secularism therefore has an inherently subjective dimension.

But there are certain objective measures of secularism which can be briefly stated: (1) in the natural world, the degree to which everything is purported to be controlled by a natural system of laws, and not by some force behind the scenes; (2) in the human personality, the degree to which what was earlier considered supernatural, or the work of spirits and demons, is now presumed to be understood scientifically, or at least will be understood when the scientific tools are sharpened enough; (3) in the realm of human values, an area long assumed to be free from scientific meddling, the degree to which the possibility exists of scientifically determining human values and meanings.

The Christian church has taken several typical stances toward the process of secularism.

1. The tight line of defense. In many ways the Roman Catholic Church has best illustrated this position, although many other smaller sect groups have also taken it. In this stance, the way to keep the secular from gaining hegemony is to define rigorously the boundaries of the sacred and secular, and to instigate means to keep the faithful from the secular. The Scholastics, the Sectarians, and many "evangelicals" have also vigorously defended Christianity against this type of secularism.

2. The "incorporationist" stance. From this point of view, that

which is considered secular and inimical to God is reinterpreted as part of God's way of doing things. Thus, when secular man discovered that the world was not the center of the universe, contrary to the biblical interpretation, the secular discovery was reinterpreted to show how much "greater" God really was. In recent times, the belief that God is "in the world" is another variant of the same stance.

3. The denial of the sacred-secular dichotomy. The Deists and other groups such as Christian Science which have stressed the need to bring all of life into the "kingdom of God" have tended to ignore the fact of the secular and to condone all things as lawful. Alternately, some groups have condemned almost all things as outside the realm of Christ and have become ascetic.

Secularism has great importance to the Christian church because it has diverted a great deal of energy that might have otherwise been used for better purposes. Secularism has further engendered a great deal of hostility and conflict, both among the members of the church and with those not subscribing to the faith. Accordingly, the church has not been as effective as it might have been in pursuing its original objectives. Secularism is a factor which the Christian church must deal with as a part of its very life and self-identification.

Population density and the technology level are two other environmental conditions which have been of great importance to Christianity. They differ from the others above in that they have been changing much more rapidly than the others.

Population density has always been significant for social structure and culture. It has been both a cause and an effect of social organization and technology. For a major part of the time that Christianity was growing, its concern was with reproduction for survival, not overpopulation. Hence, it welcomed large families and children as an insurance against population decimation through famine or plague. Population density became a problem, however, beginning with the discovery of the relationship between sanitation and health. The emergence of larger cities and concentrations of population brought problems such as crowding, breakdown of the traditional family, and increase in certain kinds of antisocial behavior.

Although in less densely populated times the social structure was more stable and traditional, the growth of populations resulted in a mobility and instability which, according to experts, has been the basis of much social disorganization. This transition has been classically described as the transition from a *Gemeinschaft* (communal) to a *Gesellschaft* (contractual) type of human relationship.

Population density alone, however, has not been responsible for this development; technology has also been instrumental. Technology has been constantly changing throughout the history of human civilization. It is the rate of change, however, which has changed. During the Christian era, technology changed slowly at first, but has been changing rapidly in recent years. It is not known where further technological change will lead, although some think civilization has almost reached the limit of technological change.

Technology, in conjunction with population increase, has brought on what can be termed "mass culture," or "mass society." Population increase and technological progress have allegedly affected social structure to such an extent that individuals have become depersonalized and human relations have become impersonal and detached, segmented, and specialized. Man's relationships have become less and less attached to small groups and associations, such as family and neighborhood groups. Increasingly, large complexes such as industry, government, and military institutions control human behavior and destiny.[25]

It is impossible to describe how populations and technology have cooperated to bring mass society into existence. However, the potential for impersonality and dehumanization has always been present; they are merely more prevalent and noticeable as human history advances.

The Christian church's stance toward population density increase has been varied and noncommittal.[26] It is well known that until just recently, the Catholic Church has taken a firm position of encouraging conception and "replenishing the

28

earth." The Protestant church, more concerned, has in the last half century come increasingly to stress limitations of population growth and density.

The stand on the development of technology is difficult to describe exactly. In many instances Christians have indicated that technology is completely moral. This position says that anything subject to development is part of God's gift to man, since God has provided the principles which can be discovered and used, and has given man the mind necessary to develop technology. Another common position is that technology is neutral, that the critical issue is how it is controlled. Thus gunpowder is neutral, but it can be used for good and evil purposes. Another stand, taken mainly by disinherited and sect groups, is that technology is dangerous to a full realization of Christian community; at best technology must be rigidly controlled if basic commitment to Christianity is not to be undercut.

The Christian church successfully evaded the problems of population density and technology until now. But the problems are getting critical and the church can no longer ignore it. Experts such as Lewis Mumford give the cities fewer than fifty years in which to rehabilitate themselves or face utter disorganization. Population experts state that unless the population explosion is stopped, the world, including the West, will be catastrophically overcrowded. The church has not been overly concerned or active in these critical areas in the past. It is an open question whether it will stir itself to action in time.

2

Social Scientists and the Critical Issues

The previous chapter presented some critical issues as seen from the perspective of a Christian sociologist. Although the perspective was more descriptive than critical, a normative position undergirded the discussion. The Christian church, it was maintained, has not been as effective as its basic teachings would require. Although this observation cannot be documented, it is a familiar thesis.

But what about thinkers who are not religiously oriented? What is the thinking of leading social scientists regarding the most crucial social issues as they see them? This question will be expanded and given more depth and substance by reporting what careful analysis from a scientific, nonreligious perspective is saying to our discussion and argument. The discussion in this chapter will rely heavily on several significant sociologists. It will also rely on a book entitled *The Sociological Tradition*,[1] by Robert Nisbet, who evaluates and classifies the thought of some leading social scientists and presents them in a very useful framework.

Nisbet considers Tocqueville, Le Play, Marx, Weber, Tännies, Durkheim, Simmel, Taine, and De Coulanges as some of the most important social thinkers in sociology. He further suggests that most of the important sociological ideas were introduced by these men, and that later contributions have been mainly expansions or elaboration of their basic ideas. "Strip from present-day sociology the perspectives and frameworks provided by men like Weber and Durkheim, and little would be left but lifeless heaps of data and stray hypotheses."[2]

Nisbet maintains that there are five unit ideas in sociological thinking — ideas which encompass most, if not all, of the various sociological concepts and concerns. These five are *community, authority, status,* the *sacred,* and *alienation.* Nisbet sees these unit ideas as the bases for most of the thinking that great social scientists have done. More surprising, however, is Nisbet's insistence that modern sociology is based on moral considerations, and that the great strides that have been made in sociology have been due to moral conscience, supported by a creative and artistic genius. In other words, the great sociological ideas originate from a moral concern, and gain their hearing when they are imaginatively conceived and presented.[3] These unit ideas can be systematically reviewed.

Community

Based on his analysis of the thinkers listed above, Nisbet concludes that "the most fundamental and far-reaching of sociology's unit ideas is community."[4] Nisbet believes that the concept of community impinges on more than sociology; that it extends into philosophy, history, and theology. The rediscovery of community, he maintains, was the greatest concern of nineteenth-century social thought and even spills over into contemporary thought.

Nisbet defines community as that which "encompasses all forms of relationship which are characterized by a high degree of personal intimacy, emotional depth, moral commitment, social cohesion, and continuity in time. Continuity is founded on man conceived in his wholeness rather than in one or another of the roles, taken separately, that he may hold in a social order."[5]

All the leading thinkers concerned with community have been motivated by the conservative view. They say that community is in danger of being lost, and that everything possible must be done in order to preserve or recapture community. Although they do not agree on what community was like or should be, most of the thinkers agree that it is to be retained if at all possible. The man best known for his position on the loss of community is Ferdinand Tönnies, but others have echoed his and similar concerns.

Tönnies proposes that human society can be described on the basis of a typology termed the "*Gemeinschaft-Gesellschaft* continuum." The term "*Gemeinschaft*" has been generally defined as "community," but this begs the question. Tönnies says that the requirement for relationships of the *Gemeinschaft* type is the natural will, normally exemplified by kinship or friendship and neighborhood. The *Gemeinschaft* relationship is most naturally described by the family.

The *Gesellschaft* relationship is based on rationality and cal-

32

culation. All activities and relationships are restricted to a definite end and to a definite means of achieving them. *Gesellschaft* is fostered in the modern economic enterprise. The city nurtures *Gesellschaft*, whereas rural areas tend to support *Gemeinschaft* relationships. The *Gemeinschaft* relationship is based on common spirit, mind, beliefs, and goals. However, the *Gesellschaft* relationship depends upon the basic heterogeneity in all things except the one factor which produces the relationship, such as the exchange of desired products.

The two types of relationships are not mutually exclusive but shade imperceptibly into each other. Tönnies devised the typology to describe degrees of individualization as over against community identification, increasing competition and egoism, increasing impersonality, increasing rationally motivated behavior, and contractualism. Tönnies clearly saw a movement from the *Gemeinschaft* to the *Gesellschaft* relationship in the history of western society. However, he did not believe that *Gesellschaft* relationships would ever completely supersede the *Gemeinschaft*, for *Gemeinschaft* relationships are imperative for the survival of society. In other words, he believed that the affective motive could never be completely eradicated in favor of the volitional, for society depends upon some affect to keep individuals in some social bond.

Tönnies sees history as marching from *Gemeinschaft* to *Gesellschaft*, with no possibility of a reversal; therefore he is no romantic. He does not disparage completely the *Gesellschaft* relationship, but feels strongly that the loss of the *Gemeinschaft* relationship is an ethical and moral issue. Because most desirable traits, such as love, loyalty, honor, friendship, and intimacy, are fostered by the *Gemeinschaft* relationship, he strongly feels that it should be strengthened wherever possible.

The other writers echo Tönnies' views, although in their own ways. Nisbet suggests, for example, that August Comte's view was one of "Community lost, community to be gained." [6] He continues, "For Comte, restoration of community is a matter of moral urgency." [7] Again the family is seen as a model for the type of relationship which ought to be obtained in

33

all social ties. Because he despised the individualism which was beginning to appear as the result of the Revolution, Comte was one of the first to emphasize the absurdity of trying to reduce society to individuals.

Comte uses the Christian feudal system as a model as far as form is concerned, but without its content. Tönnies includes the churches as *Gemeinschaft* associations, but does not see the church as keeping this relationship alive in the face of urban developments. Although Weber takes a similar position, stating that religious brotherhoods are "communal," he does not believe that Christianity, in the West, will preserve the communal type of relationship.

Emile Durkheim deserves more extensive treatment here than space permits. Durkheim stressed two grossly different types of social solidarity that could exist. In the mechanical type, tradition dominates and the individual is subordinated to the collective conscience. In the organic type of social relationship, the individual is released from the "traditional restraints of kinship, class, localism, and the generalized social conscience." [8] Durkheim also believes that religion is not the indispensable source of social solidarity, for the moral conscience has its origin in the collective conscience as well.

Thus, the idea of community is a bedrock concept determining most other social relationships. The giants of sociology started with a concern for the substantive framework of human relationships and conceptualized it in the term "community," which has an intuitive meaning for all of us even though it has been defined and operationalized in different ways. They were on the track of an important reality, for there is no other dynamic that will explain the long list of utopian schemes as well as the general quest for community. [9] The theological basis or dimension of community will be discussed later.

For our purposes here only one brief analytical observation can be made. All of the thinkers are concerned about the recapture of community, but none of them see the Christian church, in any way, as the institution by which this can be done.

34

Authority

This is the second major sociological unit idea which Nisbet discusses and which he maintains has inspired leading sociological thinkers. Authority and community obviously are closely related. The concept of community inherently involves the concept of authority. In fact, in the traditional forms of community, authority is indistinguishable from it. That is to say, the traditional forms of community are based on an intrinsic authority and therefore illustrate the interrelationship of community and authority.

It is difficult to define authority in a way that does not become partisan or specialized. Nisbet does not define it himself, although he describes the meanings that the chief sociologists give it. Power and domination are included in the concept of authority. Authority refers to the restraints on or inducement of behavior, beliefs, and feelings which are voluntarily accepted, whether the specific content of the authority is in accord with wishes of the person submitting or not. Power and domination generally mean restraints imposed in spite of resistance or reluctance.

Authority continues to be an important basic unit idea because it refers to the process or nature of individual integration into the larger society. It concerns the checking of the individual wills in favor of the group; the restraint of inordinate power of one individual or group over another. It refers to liberty and equality, rights and duties. Every group exercises authority over its members, although the form may vary tremendously. In some societies, the individual in a certain position is the lone possessor of authority, whereas in others each individual possesses certain powers which he voluntarily gives to the group.

Authority may vary also in terms of its legitimation. Some authority is legitimated by virtue of its age and tradition. Often authority is based on the qualities of the holders. Still other authority is based on rational considerations, or on the basis of a complex bureaucratic system. Authority is sometimes based on class or status devolving on those who occupy the particular class. Authority can also be described as being political, religious, or social, depending upon the institutional structure from which it emanates. The authority of the state is often said to be absolute, since it alone has the power to take a person's life without impunity, as in war or in capital punishment.

From a scientific perspective, authority is merely a descriptive concept for how a society governs itself. It is, however, a much more important concept in the thinking of most sociologists because of the value orientation from which authority is seen. That is, how a society controls its members becomes significant when a position is held on how it *ought* to govern. Here Nisbet again states that the leading sociologists made authority a cardinal idea because all of them were concerned about an erosion of authority throughout history. Although many of the thinkers disagree about what actually is happening, all are convinced that authority as it has been known and operating is breaking down.

Alexis de Tocqueville was deeply concerned about the breakdown of authority as it had traditionally been known, and its replacement by a new form which he did not think was very desirable. Tocqueville maintained that traditional authority had its roots in the medieval entities such as guild, community, and church. The aristocratic elite also possessed authority, which served to keep the lower classes under control. The closely integrated hierarchy or orders and classes in the traditional society served to put every person in a subordinate position to someone else.

The tendency for centralization of political functions in a mass democracy has tended to shift the source of authority from the traditional aristocracy to the masses, which Tocqueville feels is less desirable, since it can contribute to totalitarianism and anarchism. This undermines the autonomy of the local community association, thus enabling demagoguery to become much more effective. Tocqueville clearly was concerned about how men tend to control each other's behavior.

The other leading sociologists were similarly concerned. Only one more, Durkheim, can be briefly mentioned. For Durkheim,

36

"Authority is the bedrock of society.[10] Durkheim believes that "there is no form of social activity which can do without the appropriate moral discipline. . . . The interests of the individual are not those of the group he belongs to and, indeed, there is often a real antagonism between the one and the other."[11] Nisbet states that, for Durkheim, "Authority 'performs an important function in forming character and personality in general.' "[12]

The source of authority for Durkheim was not the state, but rather the diverse "spheres of kinship, local community, profession, church, school, guild, and labor union as well as in political government."[13] Durkheim's greatest concern was the anarchy of individualism, which seems to threaten as society changes from the traditional to the industrial. Because the individual needs the authority of a group which is superior to himself, he feels the important responsibility for social development is the encouragement of social groups competent to provide the authority the individual needs.

Neither Tocqueville nor Durkheim believes that religious groups will be able to provide the authority for individuals. Durkheim says, "religions can socialize us only insofar as they refuse us the right of free examination. They no longer have, and probably never will have again, enough authority to wring such a sacrifice from us."[14] Durkheim believes that only a primitive religion in which the individual is totally subordinated to the cult would be able to provide such an authority, but that it is impossible to expect a primitive religion ever to be reinstituted.

The concern for authority, or a basis for justifying the domination of men, is a basic one. It is a concern that impresses social thinkers as never having been solved, nor of being solved in the near future. It will not be solved because there is little agreement as to what the basis for authority should be, and what its form and content should be. Again it is interesting to note that the thinkers do not think religion can serve as the source of authority (that is, how men in groups control each other) even though some think it once was able to do so.

Status

Classes, hierarchies, orders of creation, and chains of being are concepts that have been used to describe society's universal tendency to place people in different hierarchical positions. Although it is maintained that the concept of class did not emerge until the late eighteenth century, the fact of class was present nevertheless, although it naturally was different from time to time.

The "chain of being" concept has great significance for the structure of society, for if there is a hierarchy of positions, a number of consequences follow: (1) the decision-making process is simplified since the decisions normally are made at the top and handed down; (2) responsibility is clearly allocated so that everyone knows what his individual responsibility and obligations are; (3) depending upon the rigidity of the chain, great stability and dependability are assured; (4) competition is minimized because there is usually little possibility of intra-class mobility.

At the bottom of the status class unit idea is the master-servant relationship. Where persons find themselves in different classes, one is usually the dominant and served, while the other is normally the subordinated and the servant. Tocqueville astutely suggests that there are real differences in the master-servant relationship of the classical English class system and the American class system. In American democracy, servants are "in some sort, the equals of their masters."[15]

Karl Marx, well known for his views of the class system, believes that Society is dominated by two major classes, the oppressed and the oppressor. He believes in the eternal nature of classes because he feels that once the working class has overthrown the industrialist bourgeoisie, the class struggle will still not be complete. Marx assumes that a consciousness of class will always be necessary in order to prevent exploitation by an incipient class, for consciousness of class always requires an antagonist or enemy who is "guilty." For Marx, the overriding concern is the exploitation of one class of people by another. This concern for exploitation derives from some type of ethical norm of equality most clearly derived from the Judaic-Christian tradition from which Marx sprang.

Max Weber made a significant contribution to the analysis of class in suggesting that the concept of class be limited to the purely economic activities in which human beings engage. Weber says class refers to the "life chances" of individuals as they compete for goods and opportunities of income in the economic level. Weber does not believe a class "interest" or consciousness could develop, since that would amount to the same concept as community. Although Weber does not talk about exploitation in this context, he does talk about competition and domination. In distinguishing the concept of status from class, Weber suggests that status groups are usually communities, and that the position accorded them is based on some type of social honor or esteem.[16]

One of the more important contributions of Weber's analysis is the way status groups can become caste groups. In this process, the concept of social honor and dignity determines the development of "styles of life" which exclude interaction to outsiders. The style of life is created by belonging to the "inner circle" rather than by strict ownership of property. Thus, according to Weber, stratification is more usurpation of honor than it is the expression of an economic class struggle, as seen by Marx.

The theorists' concern about class and status revolves around the concept of superior and inferior peoples. The concept of an elite and a proletariat has tempted many societies. The existence of an aristocracy above the masses has been defended for much of human history, especially by those in the upper class. Many social structures have evidenced the concept of superior and inferior classes. The extended family, with its distinctions between the family proper and the servants, is evidence of it. Within the family itself, the superiority of the oldest members over the younger and of the parents over the children further delineates this principle.

The class structure has existed in many societies, often seemingly without much trouble. But others illustrate less acquiescence. The Indian caste system exemplifies the former, whereas the South African system depends upon police enforcement. Georg Simmel suggests that "typically speaking, nobody is satisfied with the position he occupies in regard to his fellow creatures; everybody wishes to attain one which is, in some sense, more favorable. . . . Equality with the superior is the first objective which offers itself to the impulse of one's own elevation."[17]

Many justifications have been offered for the maintenance of a class and status system. One is that the privileged upper class are superior; thus, the ruled need to be satisfied with their being on top. Another is that being a part of the elite is no privilege, but rather a chore; that the inferiors need to be happy for what the superiors do for them in terms of setting the cultural milieu and cultural amenities. One other justification is that those on top have gotten there by hard work, and that everyone who wants to become a member of the elite must do likewise.

Obviously, members of the lower class have typically denied the truth of the supposed justifications, or have ignored them and taken an attitude of resignation and fatalism toward their own chances of moving upward. And, of course, most sociologists including the ones referred to above have concluded that religion (in this case, Christianity) has done little to intervene in the class-status question. Indeed, overwhelming evidence suggests that the Christian church has not destroyed class and status differences, but has rather been a defender and a protector of class distinctions.[18]

Sacred-Secular

Nisbet suggests that the concept of the sacred (i.e., the broad human experience of religion) is unique to the sociological discipline, and thus provides a unique perspective for analyzing human institutions.[19] Nisbet further suggests that the understanding of the sacred as used in understanding the non-sacred institutions enables sociology to make an advance not available to the other social disciplines.

Although religion has become increasingly disdained by philosophers, artists, and others, the sociologists have become increasingly impressed with the role of the sacred in human affairs. And although most sociologists have demurred as far as taking a position on the objective reality of religion is concerned, they have agreed that, illusory or not, religion has a function in society which cannot be ignored. In the earliest societies which were entirely filled with sacred aspects, it is impossible to analyze the society without describing it as a religious system. In the more advanced societies, religions have become increasingly "split off" so that the interrelationship between society and religion is even more complex.[20]

For the sociologist, religion or the sacred has been one of the most important considerations because of the role religion plays in the life of any society. The perspective of the thinker, of course, makes all the difference as to the role that he gives to religion. For Marx, religion is the most colossal brainwashing job ever brought off by man. On the other extreme, Fustel De Coulanges in *The Ancient City* says, according to Nisbet, that "it was belief in the sacred properties of certain aspects of the environment that led to a distinctive social system. And it is, equally, the disintegration of this social system that results in profound changes in belief."[21] According to De Coulanges, religion was the central nerve of all of the pre-modern social structure.

Of all recent scholars, Emile Durkheim has probably made the most sweeping claims for the sacred. He maintains that the dichotomy between the sacred and profane is central to all religion. It is evidenced in the fact that societies have always acknowledged a "holy" and an "ordinary." Religion always has a church, and the church is the social group in which the religion is practiced. For Durkheim religion is the most important process by which society gains the transcendence over the individual in society. Religion is the ritualistic process by which the group or society objectifies itself and creates a system of goals and commensurate authority by which individuals are brought into a binding relationship with the whole.

Simmel shares in some measure Durkheim's view of religion.

He suggests that in the social relationship itself there is something religious and mysterious. The emotional responses to human social relationships produce a kind of frame of mind, or piety. Without piety, society would be impossible, Simmel maintains, for the selfless devotion to others, for example, would not survive in the absence of piety.[22]

Of the numerous other views of what religion does in the social fabric, only one more general orientation can be included, namely, functionalism. Functionalism does not bother to evaluate religion in an ontological or metaphysical sense. Rather, it asks in a matter of fact way, "What does the institution of religion do in any society?" The results of the inquiry have pointed to the integrating factor that religion plays. That is, religion performs the function of harmonizing the values, goals, and aspirations of people. It further serves to bridge the gap in a society between its aspirations and its accomplishments. Religion often has been seen as providing an explanation for suffering and undeserved experiences, as well as death. It also has been said to be the most important provider of the goals of a society.

As indicated in chapter 1, there is less agreement than ever before as to the nature of religion. As a result, the study of religion is taking increasingly the form of gathering massive amounts of data on attitudes, beliefs, and behavior of religion. In fact, most sociologists now are not really very much concerned about the ultimate nature and meaning of religion. In this attitude they are straying from the titans of sociology who were deeply concerned about the nature of religion and its relation to society. In any case, religion cannot be ignored, as Davis says:

> Religion, then, does four things that help to maintain the dominance of sentiment over organic desire, of group ends over private interest. First, it offers, through its system of supernatural belief, an explanation of the group ends and a justification of their primacy. Second, it provides, through its collective ritual, a means for the constant renewal of the common sentiments. Third, it furnishes, through its sacred objects, a concrete reference for the values and a

rallying point for all persons who share the same values. Fourth, it provides an unlimited and insuperable source of rewards and punishments — rewards for good conduct, punishment for bad. In these ways religion makes a unique and indispensable contribution to social integration.[23]

Some students of religion maintain that religion is indispensable for the functioning of human society. Others have rejected this position. What most social scientists agree upon is that religion performs functions for the survival of society, for which no real alternatives are available at present. They do not say, however, that alternatives will never be found, but that at the present time it is impossible for any other institution to take over all the functions that religion now performs. Many others seriously doubt whether any institution will ever take over all the functions that religion has performed in the past.

Alienation

Nisbet maintains that the concept of alienation is recent, having been popularized by Karl Marx.[24] Nisbet recognizes two dimensions or perspectives of alienation, the first one being "an alienated view of the individual, the second one an alienated view of society."[25] According to the first, "we see modern man as uprooted, alone, without secure status, cut off from community or any system of clear moral purpose."[26] According to to the second, "modern society is inaccessible because of its remoteness, formidable from its heavy structures of organization, meaninglessness from its impersonal complexity."[27]

A definition of alienation cannot be given which will do justice to all the men who have thought about it; so only a very general view is possible. At the heart of the concern voiced regarding alienation is what the process of social change is doing to the individual. For some thinkers increasing individualism has separated the person from his social and moral moorings and has made him an unrelated and drifting object. Others are concerned about what the increasing bureaucratization and massification might do to the individual's self-understanding and integrity. The increasing impersonalization of the metropolis threatens to deprive the individual of the many rich relationships he had enjoyed earlier. Tocqueville states:

> When I survey this countless multitude of beings, shaped in each other's likeness, amid whom nothing rises and nothing falls, the sight of such universal uniformity saddens and chills me and I am tempted to regret the state of society which has ceased to be. . . . [28]

The individual dimension of alienation refers to the loss of purpose, wholeness, identity, and integrity that are presumed either to have existed earlier, or to be the desired goals of the person. Individual meaningful existence is the opposite of alienation, which is said to be disappearing.

In the societal dimension of alienation, the individual is not meaningfully related to a social group and is therefore not restrained by a group which has a coherent set of norms, goals, and beliefs. The morale of the group and of the individuals belonging to it has deteriorated so that there is no feeling of belonging, of common purpose, common commitment, and common motivation. The absence of meaningful ties to society is the thermometer of social alienation. One technical treatment describes the two forms of alienation as follows: " . . . (1) social alienation — in which individual selves may find the social system in which they live to be oppressive or incompatible with some of their own desires and feel estranged from it; and (2) self-alienation — in which individual selves may lose contact with any inclinations or desires that are not in agreement with prevailing social patterns, manipulate their selves in accordance with apparent social demands, and/or feel incapable of controlling their own actions."[29]

Clearly, total individualism and absolute group conformity, taken as polar extremes, are equal cases of alienation, for in both the individual is not whole nor is his relationship to a group meaningful and complete. The results of alienation include individual behavior such as inactivity, directionless activity, mental illness, and, at worst, suicide. On a group level alienation evidences itself in individuals not relating to social groups and institutions. Instead, individuals are intentionally disregarding social norms and severing their group relationships in order to follow their own whims and wishes, in order not to be disciplined and restrained by them.

Alienation is not easy to define and test. It is easy to document scientifically the birth rate or suicide rate, but to use these rates or any others to infer alienation is another matter. In any case, the more impassioned the thinkers were, the more they were concerned about the alienation of man. The consequences of these concerns have been momentous, as in the results of Marx's use of the concept of alienation to explain how man must be reunited with his environment in order for the kingdom of man to become reality. Max Weber expressed himself most somberly in reflecting on the possibility of complete alienation:

> Not summer's bloom lies ahead of us, but rather a polar night of icy darkness and hardness. When this night shall have slowly receded, who of those for whom Spring apparently has bloomed so luxuriously will be alive?[30]

One of the most astounding conclusions a student of alienation comes to is that religion, and in our case, Christianity, is not referred to in the literature as being the antidote for alienation. This in the face of the basic tenet that Christianity has come to bring atonement, or at-one-ment with God and with his fellowman.

Nisbet does not maintain categorically that these unit ideas are the final ideas concerning social life, but he believes that, at least until now, these have been effective tools for the analysis of our condition, and suggests that no really promising, new conceptualizations are appearing on the horizon. He suggests, however, that a new and more useful conceptualization (if that is indeed possible) will come not by sterile data gathering, but by "passion for reality that is direct and unmediated."[31] Since none have appeared so far, one can safely assume that the passion for reality described by these leading thinkers has fairly well defined the conditions of our time. Religion, especially Christianity, has not been given very good grades, in terms of its potentiality for solving the basic predicament of modern times, and has its job cut out for itself!

3

The Seduction
of the
Christian Church

It is easy, although painful, to show that the Christian church has not yet realized its true potential, even though our definitions of what the true potential should be may vary. The basic question therefore before us is this: What is the relationship between Christianity and the society in which it exists? (A) Is the Christian religion really independent of the society in which it exists? (B) Is the Christian religion transcendental in origin but constantly changed through its involvement in social existence (although it also changes society in the process)? (C) Or is the Christian religion a product of society and also an expression of it?[1]

Most social scientists would choose the last option, even though they would say that once religion has emerged, it develops an autonomy and force of its own. Some ascetics and pietistically oriented people would take the first option, but a vast majority of Christians would take the second. In fact, theologians insist that in its deepest sense the incarnation means a transcendental phenomenon becoming somehow related to the mundane existence, changing it and being changed by it. But the crux of the question is: How much must and can the Christian gospel be changed in the incarnation before it loses its essence? The dilemma has been ably stated by Christopher Dawson:

> Any religious movement which adopts a purely critical and negative attitude to culture is therefore a force of destruction and disintegration which mobilizes against it the healthiest and most constructive elements in society — elements which can by no means be dismissed as worthless from the religious point of view. On the other hand, the identification of religion with the particular cultural synthesis which has been achieved as a definite point of time and space by the action of historical forces is fatal to the universal character of religious truth.[2]

The most important question for Christianity, therefore, in the light of its promise and the world's needs, is this: Has the Christian church moved so far toward option three that it has lost its transcendent nature and has become a mere reflection of society? The thesis of this chapter, and its expli-

47

cation in the remainder of the volume, maintains that the Christian church has failed to be the true incarnation because it has moved so far in identification with culture that it is an expression of it. It has moved from option B to C in the following diagram:

Figure 1

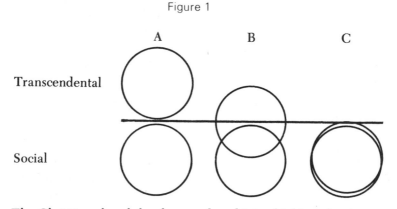

The Christian church has been seduced into thinking that its social form is its transcendental nature. This is the most tragic type of false consciousness conceivable.

Almost a half century ago, Ernst Troeltsch said, "The relation of a religious system to civilisation is always very complicated."[3] Although he was a committed Protestant Christian, he had his doubts that Protestantism would fare better than Catholicism in being the channel of the gospel of Christ. Troeltsch analyzes the nature of the *Corpus Christianum* (that period when the entire society was dominated by the Christian structure and theology) with the following concern:

> Even the civilisation of the Middle Ages was special in its character, strongly influenced by nonreligious circumstances; and if through the spiritual influence of the church it became a specifically ecclesiastical civilisation, that was due to the peculiarly complete and logical way in which absolute, saving truths were built up into an all-embracing hierarchic power.[4]

But Troeltsch seems to have already seen clearly that Protestantism as well as Catholicism was predestined to be controlled and
determined by civilization. He states:

> The real and ultimate question regarding the significance
> of Protestantism for the modern world is, therefore, in what
> relation its religious energy and fundamental principle
> stand to the religious character of the modern spirit. . . .[5]

Troeltsch's basic premise is that religion is (or at least should
be) autonomous, "and the results of its influence are really in
the first place, religious. Religion becomes a power in ordinary life only by taking up civilization into itself and giving it
a special direction. But it always itself remains distinct from this
civilization . . . it possesses the capacity to mould other
things without becoming identified with them, and to adapt itself to their changes without losing its character."[6]

Even before Troeltsch, however, there were more agonized
warnings that Protestantism will not be able to resist being
influenced and determined by civilization. In 1855 Soren Kierkegaard said:

> In the magnificent cathedral the Honorable and Right Rev-
> erend Geheime-General-Ober-Hof-Prädikant, the elect fa-
> vorite of the fashionable world, appears before an elect
> company and preaches with emotion upon the text he him-
> self elected: "God hath elected the base things of the
> world, and the things that are despised" — and nobody
> laughs.[7]

What about the Christian religion? Has the Christian religion
really been seduced by its lover, the world? The basis from
which this question can be answered remains problematical,
and will be referred to in chapter 5.

But there is considerable weight in objective facts to say that
the evidence is incontrovertible. An account of the Thirty Years'
War suggests that that was "the most horrible military episode
in Western history prior to the twentieth century."[8] An ac-
quaintance with European history will remind the reader that it
was a war fought on the question of the territorial designation
of religion. That is, it was a war fought to determine whether a
territory should be designated Catholic or Protestant. The recent

49

recurrent battle between the Protestants and Catholics in Northern Ireland illustrates the problem in a doubly tragic sense: (1) that Protestants and Catholics can still confront each other with arms and (2) that the conflict is so much more complicated due to the "corruption" of the issue through the infiltration of cultural, political, and "tribal" factors into a "religious" conflict.

In commenting on the causes and results of the Thirty Years' War, Bainton says, "But something at any rate had been gained. The principle of ecclesiastical solidarity was broken."[9]

Thus, tacit approval of a principle being gained at the expense of the slaughter of thousands of persons reflects the confused understanding of the relation of religion and human society, even by a distinguished church historian. The purpose of this chapter is to show how the Christian church tends to become the unconscious victim of and conditioned by the environment, or "civilization," to use Troeltsch's term, and to show what consequence this has for the Christian gospel.

Or to state the problem another way, the purpose is to show how the church has almost consistently suffered from the "fallacy of misplaced concretion." This fallacy is the process whereby a person or group mistakes a spurious objective, idea, or thing for the genuine or authentic reality. The fallacy is everywhere present, and may be domestically illustrated by the man who skimps and saves all his life for the future, but dies without ever entering it.

One of the first sagacious descriptions of the fallacy came from the lips of Jesus as found in Matthew 23:23, 24:

> Alas for you, lawyers and Pharisees, hypocrites! You pay tithes of mint and dill and cummin; but you have overlooked the weightier demands of the Law, justice, mercy, and good faith. It is these you should have practised, without neglecting the others. Blind guides! You strain off a midge, yet gulp down a camel!

Jesus had ample reason to speak in such terms. The history of the Jewish people had been populated with Jeremiahs protesting the "whoring after strange gods." One of the most impressive

50

and poignant examples is the prophet Hosea. According to Hosea, Israel was grossly mistaken about the causes for its troubles. He says in chapter 5, "Hear this, O Priests! Give heed, O House of Israel. Hearken, O House of the King. For the judgment pertains to you, for you have been a snare at Mizpah, and a net spread upon Tabor."

The idolatry of Israel, the "going after strange gods," rather than remaining God's faithful covenant people, is the basis for some most impressive dialogue between God and His people through the words of Isaiah and Jeremiah, Hosea and other prophets. Jesus was concerned about the same problem of "going after strange gods." The fallacy of misplaced concretion has plagued the children of Israel, the followers of Christ, the early Christian church, and continues to plague contemporary Christendom.

It is impossible to deal with the seduction of the church in any comprehensive form; hence only an example which will be prototypic and thus useful in its heuristic aspects will be employed. The Crusades of the eleventh, twelfth, and thirteenth centuries will serve as this example, since it will be less threatening to contemporary Christians. Hopefully the point can thus be made, and with raising few defenses.

The Crusades are known throughout the world as a part of the history of the Christian church as well as of secular history. With the passage of time they have acquired an aura of charm and romance. Thus H. G. Wells says:

> The story of the crusades abounds in such romantic and picturesque detail that the writer of an Outline of History must ride his pen upon the curb through this alluring field.[10]

The student of history learns about the Crusades as evidence of piety and honor on the part of kings, princes, knights, lords, and simple peasants, and fits this into his general scheme of the "alluring" medieval world.

However, serious ecclesiastical and historical analysis also gives to the Crusades a positive evaluation which matches the romantic. Louis Brehier, Professor of Ancient and Medieval

History, states:

> If indeed, the Christian civilization of Europe has become
> universal culture, in the highest sense, the glory redounds,
> in no small measure, to the Crusades. [11]

The pleasant and lofty aspects of the Crusades, such as the ones
cited above, have been emphasized to the neglect of the brutality, bloodshed, and depravity which actually surrounded the
Crusades.

Not all scholars have unconditionally lauded the Crusades. In
fact, many have been appalled by what the Crusades implied
for the Christian church. One author's evaluation lists as many
negative effects of the Crusades as positive ones, and suggests
that the Crusades destroyed the Byzantine civilization, enabled
the military triumph of Islam, and inculcated an intolerance and
brutality into Western Christendom which has not yet been
exorcised. [12] The concern is not, however, to decry the Crusades, although that is necessary, but to describe them in terms
of the thesis and analyze this development. A brief description
of the Crusades will be necessary for our analysis.

The Crusades comprise a formidable segment of Christian
history and derive their original animus from pilgrimages of the
faithful to Jerusalem and the Holy Sepulchre. As early as 800
an agreement was reached with the Caliph of Bagdad for the
keys to the Holy Sepulchre. Churches and monasteries were
built and Christian communities developed in support of the
worship at the holy places. The sudden destruction of the Holy
Sepulchre and the destruction of the Christian communities in
1009 by Hakem, the Fatimate Caliph of Egypt, upset the understanding and mutual toleration that had existed and precipitated the demands for the recovery of the Holy East for
western Christians.

The consequent persecution of the Christian pilgrims by
the Turks and the capture of Jerusalem in 1070 marked the
beginning of extreme agitation in Europe. Pope Urban II has
been credited with instigating the Crusades at a council at
Clermont-Ferraud in Auvergne. To his stirring message calling for a rescue of the Holy Sepulchre, the assembled arch-

bishops, bishops, abbots, knights, and commoners responded by shouting *Deus Vult* ("God wills it"). Simultaneously the pope sent letters to all the "Christian nations" asking for help. A mass response whose consequences almost defy the imagination took place in Europe.

One account describes the mass frenzy as follows:

> Preachers of the crusades appeared everywhere, and on all sides sprang up disorganized, undisciplined, penniless hordes, almost destitute of equipment, who, surging eastward through the valley of Danube, plundered as they went along and murdered the Jews in German cities.[13]

The Crusades cannot be fully comprehended short of an extensive treatment as has been given in *A History of the Crusades* in five volumes edited by K. M. Setton and others.[14] But the complexity of the motives, issues, multiplicity of conflicting leadership, and the general chaos of the Crusades must at least be alluded to. There were eight crusades if a narrow definition of the Crusades is used.

The First Crusade began in 1096 and resulted in the taking of Jerusalem and environs and their control until 1109. A part of the First Crusade involved conflict with the Eastern Church, which had severed itself from the western branch in 1054. The pope had hoped that both branches of the church would unite in fighting a common enemy. However, the attempt at political and ecclesiastical unification proved fruitless, and hope for any unified action was dashed.

The Second Crusade was precipitated by the seizure of Aleppo in 1128 by Imad-al-Din and created such disorder between the Turks and the Franks (the name given to all the Crusaders) that the Muslims began to reassert their open hostility upon the Franks. Hence Pope Eugenius III issued a call for the second crusade. This crusade was less successful than the first, largely because of the lack of support from the Byzantine Empire, and ended in disaster in 1148. By this defeat, the Turks lost the respect and fear of the Europeans that they had earlier had, which served to stem the tide from that point on of European domination in the Holy Land.

The Third Crusade, called by Pope Gregory VIII and his successor Clement III, commissioned Frederick of Barbarossa in 1189. His drowning in the Saleph River on June 10, 1190, initiated the gradual breakdown of the crusade, even though a war-loving Richard of England tried to salvage it. A Fourth Crusade, dedicated to salvaging prestige, was vowed by French nobles and blessed by Innocent III, but because of fortuitous events, it was only able to reach Constantinople. The conflict between the pope and the Byzantine imperial throne reached the breaking point with the crusaders' siege of that city.

The Fifth Crusade, called by Honorius III, was organized in 1218. This crusade attacked Damietta in Egypt first and would probably have been successful had it not been for the loss of Cardinal Pelagius' army in a Nile flood. By the Sixth Crusade (1227) morale was so low and feelings so bitter that civil war developed among the Franks, and the Sultan of Egypt was able to capture Frankish Palestine and Damascus.

The Seventh Crusade, launched by Louis IX of France, followed the strategy of the Fifth Crusade and attacked Damietta, Egypt. The results were so inconsequential that Louis took to negotiations, which were not eagerly accepted by the church or by the princes. The Eighth Crusade was also launched by Louis in 1267. Because of a conflict with his brother Charles, Louis was diverted to Tunisia, which allowed the Sultan of Egypt, Qutuz, to complete the capture of all of the Holy Land for the Muslim faith.

There were lingering attempts to revive the Crusades until 1571. As a matter of historical interest, the explorations of Prince Henry the Navigator, Christopher Columbus, and Alfonso d'Albuquerque "all solemnly claimed that their voyages of discovery would circumvent the Muslims of the eastern Mediterranean,"[15] and thus allow the nations to rearm for the final defeat of the infidel.

It is impossible to understand the Crusades except by seeing them as an expression of an entire society in convulsion, with the Christian church giving society such form and theology as it had. That this mass movement reached from the top of

54

the chain of being to the bottom is illustrated in the following observation:

> Now as time passed, with the obvious failure of knightly arms to free Jerusalem, the idea that the meek might do what the proud and mighty had been unable to do all the more possessed the minds of lesser folk.[16]

Only two instances of the crowd psychology and confusion that obtained can be given. The first is the Children's Crusade which, although it had many spontaneous sources of origin, is reputed to have been started by a young shepherd of Vendome. Thousands of children gathered at various places and began to march to the Holy Land to free Jerusalem from the infidel. By the time the "army" reached Italy it was throughly demoralized. Many were sold as slaves to the Moors, according to some evidence, while many others died of starvation and exhaustion. The astounding thing is not that a young segment of society could be caught up in the mass hysteria, but that no saner heads in the church could prevail to prevent the children from walking into the valley of death.

The other brief account which alludes to the confusion and frenzy of the Crusades involves the description of conditions after the Turks finally ejected the Franks from the Holy City.

> No longer aided by funds from the West, and rent by internal disorders, the Christian colonies owed their temporary salvation to the changes in Mussulman policy and the intervention of the Mongols. The Venetians drove the Genoese from Saint Jean D'Arcre and treated the city as conquered territory in a battle where Christians fought against Christians, and in which Hospitallers were pitted against Templars, 20,000 perished.[17]

This author seems scandalized that Christians should fight fellow Christians, as if this were the bad side of the Crusades. More will be said about this later. But the suffering, torture, disease, starvation, carnage, and death created by the Crusades are not normally discussed and evaluated in the descriptions of the Crusades. And if they are, they are discussed in unemotional terms somewhat like the "body counts" in modern war reports, insulated from the population which supports these wars.

The Crusades are but one example of the "seduction" of the Christian church. As was indicated above, many examples could be cited that illustrate the captivity of the Christian church by the "spirit of the age." Since the development of the scientific social science research, numerous studies have been conducted which provide concrete descriptions of the ways in which the Christian church has been molded by its environment. A study typical of this development, and representative in its devastating judgment on the Christian church is Gibson Winter's *The Suburban Captivity of the Churches*.[18] The basic thrust of the book is that "The churches could play a significant role in metropolitan planning, and yet, for the most part, they have failed to participate responsibly in the metropolis."[19] At another point he speaks of the "religious betrayal of the metropolis."[20]

Although this and other studies use other language, the reference is the same — the Christian church has failed to carry out its mission. In the case of Winter's analysis, the failure is the lack of providing an orderly integration of "sectors" of life in the city. Instead of providing an integration of the various interests, classes, and power, the Christian church has been one of the major causes of urban ethnic, racial, and socio-economic cleavages. The conceptual analysis may vary, but the concern seems to be the same. The question of why the Christian church has "failed" is not answered on the same level of clarity as the analysis of the failure. This is the concern to which we are addressing ourselves in this study.

In a part of the Sermon on the Mount, Jesus said, "So, if your eye is sound, your whole body will be full of light; but if your eye is not sound, your whole body will be full of darkness" (Matthew 6:22). The achievement of the "sound eye" is not simple. It might be said that the Christians who participated in the Crusades had a single-minded devotion to Christ. Many would reject this interpretation and say that the Crusades were monstrously "unsound" and diabolical illustrations of the fallacy of misplaced concretion. But no one of us is free from being of unsound eyes, of having our vision darkened. We all have "blind spots" in the way in which we perceive reality. All of us have our "crusades" in which we misperceive the false for the real.

Does this mean that everybody is a possessor of "unsound eyes" and sees the world from a twisted perspective? The answer is yes. Complete objectivity has been forsaken as an ideal ever since the psychological revolution, which culminated in the theory of the subconscious by Freud. We know that man is no longer a purely rational animal, if he ever was. He is motivated by a murky reservoir of unconscious drives and forces. Although he is able to ratiocinate, he is prone to "bend" his cognitive processes to align with the forces not related to the objective situation.[21]

But the other side must not be forgotten, namely, that man is able to apprehend the external reality relatively unbiased, at least at certain times and in certain situations. That is to say, man is often able to see the fallacy in his own cognitive processes, either on his own, or when it is pointed out to him. For example, a husband can receive some insight from a counselor about his own attitudes and behavior which will help him in his relationships to his wife, if his wife indeed cannot help him. This ability to perceive at least some aspects of reality objectively and accurately has been claimed by Karl Mannheim.[22]

Groups as well as individuals can be the victims of particular ideology, in which they tend to see external reality biased in favor of the group's position. This has many designations: ethnocentrism, nationalism, chauvinism, group egoism, and others. Groups or societies can misperceive objective reality so that they are unaware of their deceptive perception of reality. A painful, but real illustration would be the way the United States perceives itself as the protector of all that is good and the communist world as the personification of all that is diabolical.

However, groups that succumb to particular ideology are

able also to be released from this captivity. A national blind spot can be removed when objective circumstances can no longer be "explained away." Thus the German super-nation ideology was largely removed when World War II in all its horror reduced the nation to a pitiful ruin. The German nation underwent a thorough change and began to see itself as a gangster nation rather than as the savior of Europe. This is not to imply that Germany may not one day resume its traditional role, but for a time the national mood was drastically shaken.

What happens, however, when an individual or group is totally mistaken in its cognition of objective reality? What can be done with the person who lives in a completely false reality, as the schizophrenic does? Everything that happens to a victim of "total ideology" corroborates his cognition. Thus, for the extreme paranoid person, everything anyone tries to do to help him is seen as conspiracy, whereas anything of a negative type which he experiences substantiates his persecuted view of life. The person whose perception of objective reality is totally false interprets all symbols, feelings, and activities by his own screening grid.

Groups and societies can also totally misunderstand their objective environment, and be totally unaware of their false perceptions. Karl Marx, of course, believed that western capitalist society was a vast ideology, but not totally so because the bourgeoisie was partially aware of what they were doing to the masses. He deemed it his mission to open the eyes of the proletariat. Are there examples of groups who have been totally false in their perceptions? The western man would be quick to say that communism is itself a total ideology. He would cite Cuba as an example of a nation that is totally "duped" as far as its objective situation is concerned.

These assertions cannot be unequivocally held. There are some "objective factors" which communism has pointed to that are objectively real — for example, the exploitation of the lower social groups by the wealthy. Cuba has made some vast improvements in its economic system. On the contrary, the congenital inability of the United States to perceive its own involvement in international exploitation and its cavalier treatment of nations in Latin America could be cited just as easily as total ideologies.

But these illustrations do not come as close to total ideology as one of the most important movements of all time — Christianity! Christianity, the gospel of love, peace, equality, and brotherhood, has on the contrary perpetuated (or at least been associated with) some of the most pernicious activities in history — pernicious because these actions run completely contrary to its own teachings and charter. Therefore, if a movement can preach and proclaim peace, but engage in violence, there is no other alternative than to term it a total ideology, a totally false and misplaced understanding of itself and the objective reality.

The history of Christianity offers a study in total ideology — preaching one thing, but living in a manner which indicates that it is living in a completely falsified "objective reality." This general cynicism about Christianity has been forcefully stated by an atheist who is reputed to have said something like "I think Christianity has the answer to the world's problems. Why doesn't somebody try it?" The vast, perennial tirade against Christianity attests to this realization. The Christian religion has become a total ideology just as the Pharisees were, who according to Christ were "whited sepulchres," having the appearance of one thing, but being in reality the exact opposite.

A closer look at the Crusades shows how Christianity could become a victim of total ideology. The Crusades must be seen as taking place in time and in social space; that is, as having been determined by the social conditions in which they existed.[23]

A. The Structure of the Church

The administrative organization of the Christian church allowed mainly a one-way direction in communication and influence. The church hierarchy was a bureaucracy which permitted little reverse communication from the bottom up. The parishioner could say little to the priest; the priest had little to say to his bishop; the bishop answered and took orders from the pope. There was little feedback, something which is now considered imperative in any type of organizational structure. The church's rationale and theological premise for this one-way communication system was that the masses were illiterate; that the theologizing process should be limited to the "church," which in reality meant the clergy and church councils. To this, two answers must be given: (1) an existing condition (illiteracy) is no justification for allowing it to continue to exist; (2) the belief that only some must be allowed to interpret truth is itself an aspect of ideology and contrary to the gospel.

B. The Hierarchical System of Authority

When communication corresponds to the structure just described, then hierarchical structure is almost certain to become arbitrary and unresponsive to the situation which it meets. This expresses itself in a number of ways. 1. The higher levels of organization tend to lose touch with the lower levels. That is, the upper strata do not know how the others think, feel, and respond in relation to common events. 2. The lower echelon members tend to feel alienated and estranged from the superiors and impute motives to them which may be misunderstood or even false. 3. The activities and objectives of the organization begin to have different meanings and implications for the superiors and the subordinates. Thus they interpret each situation and event differently. 4. The officeholders in a bureaucratic structure tend to put their own positions ahead of the purpose for which the office was set up. In the church it was not uncommon for the church official to safeguard and, if possible, to enhance his position at the expense of the people whom he was to serve.

C. The Symbolic System of the Church

The system of symbolism which developed in the Catholic Church palpably contributed to the development of a total ideology. The symbols of hell, purgatory, evil spirits, angels, penance, indulgences, the cross and lamb, blood sacrifice, and others, to say nothing of the pageantry during holy days, contributed to the development of a mood, mentality, and cognitive process which could conceive of a "conquering cross" as being true to the message of Christ. A symbolic system which includes symbols such as swords, soldiers, armies, crosses, martyrs, and judgment clearly tends to produce a receptivity to accepting violence as a part of the "system of reality." Further concepts and symbols, such as truth and heresy, produced a readiness to participate in exterminating such undesirable things, and thus to achieve the desirable status of faithfulness and orthodoxy.

D. The Integration of the Church and the Socio-economic Order

Because the Catholic Church was thoroughly integrated into the economic and social environment, what took place in the "secular" environment was of great consequence for the church, if not caused by the church. Politically, the Roman Catholic Church was deeply involved in the development of Europe. The Italian scene especially was the child of the political might of the church, but the so-called "Holy Roman Empire" was also in many ways "mothered" by the Catholic Church.

> As the barbarian races settled and became Christian, the pope began to claim an overlordship of their kings. In a few centuries the pope had become in theory, and to a certain extent in practice, the high priest, censor, judge, and divine monarch of Christendom; his influence extended in the west far beyond the utmost range of the old empire, to Ireland, Norway and Sweden, and all over Germany. . . . The history of Europe from the fifth century onward to the fifteenth is very largely the history of the failure of this great idea of a divine world government to realize itself in practice.[24]

The wars fought in the name of the church and the practice of crowning the emperor are other evidences of the merger of the "cross and the crown."

Economically, the church was deeply implicated. Not only did the parishes levy taxes on the landowners in the area, but the parishes themselves owned vast amounts of property, and often priests were actively involved in economic activities of various kinds, from making wines to lending money and operating banks. Some scholars estimate that at times in Germany and France the church owned up to one half of the land. The excesses and anomalies that this produced need not be recounted here. Speaking of parish priests in the Middle Ages, Kenneth Scott Latourette says, "Indeed, avarice was one of the main charges leveled against them."[25]

When the chaotic conditions of Europe are considered, economic and political integration can easily be defended. It can be said that the church contributed to Europe's emerging stability rather than to its downfall. This again cannot be denied, but when the true objectives and purposes of the Christian church are considered, the subjection and deprivation of the masses cannot be condoned under any circumstances.

E. The Theology of the Church

Although theology is considered by the social scientist to be largely a consequence of social conditions, it is possible to consider it as a separate force contributing to the Crusades. The development of a theology of the "City of God" to be built here on earth by human hands was slow in coming, but it developed clearly and inexorably. Augustine's *City of God* and its delineation of a just war, plus the various church councils that defined what the Christian church was allowed to do, perpetuated and increased a theology of "expansion" and aggressive "Christianization" of pagans wherever they were to be found. Of course the winsomeness of the gospel was to be preeminent, but if that did not work the heresy-hunting course could always be taken. The years between 950 and 1350 saw vigorous deviance from orthodoxy, and resulted in equally vigorous repression of heresy. This reached such heights that at least on one occasion, the faithful and heretics were slaughtered alike, since it was difficult to distinguish them. The action was justified because "God knows His own."[26]

A careful look at Christian theology reveals that beliefs do make a difference in action. Therefore, a belief that the church was doing a heretic a favor for his life in the next world by slaughtering him if necessary had direct consequences for the crusading spirit that seemed to permeate the church for a number of centuries. Since theology, however, is always a child of its age, it is not just to blame theology alone. Rather, the context in which the entire *Weltanschauung* developed is the cause for the theology. The belief in spirits; the belief that men were better off dead than to potentially suffer eternal damnation; the belief that some men by virtue of their position in the chain of being were able to impose their authority and ideas on others — these were some of the factors which contributed to a theology that could support heresy-hunting, crusades, and wars of conquest for the church.

We have seen that a number of factors have been responsible for allowing the church at a certain point in its development to engage upon crusades as a response to *Deus Vult*.[27] These factors included the structure of the church, which encouraged only one-way communication; the authority structure, which set the various officials against each other; the symbolic system, which encouraged a type of "coercive mentality"; the integration of the church into the socio-economic life so that it was more concerned with its power and position than with its role as a prophet; and the theology of coercion, which presumed to determine thought, belief, and action for the masses under the church's control.

In this analysis of the factors in the structure of the Christian church that contributed to the seduction of the Crusades, a one-sided view may have been presented. That is to say, it could easily be remonstrated that the Roman Catholic Church should not be made to bear all the blame for the Crusades. It could be argued that expecting the church to behave differently simply ignores all the complexities of the social-cultural-religious conditions in which the Crusades took place.

From a sociological perspective, the Crusades could be nicely described as the product of the times. After all, the force of a thousand years of cultural development cannot be so easily sloughed off. And the Christian church was only a part of this entire development. But this is precisely the point. Granting that the Christian church was under the burden of many centuries of cultural accretions at the time of the Crusades, the

63

church failed to recognize that at each point in the history of Europe, it was helping to forge the culture that could eventually erupt in a crusading mentality.

The church thus became involved in an activity totally contrary to its mandate, and about which it was totally unconcerned. Although there were voices and consciences in opposition, the Crusades lasted over two hundred years (1096-1291).[28] The crusading spirit had become entrenched and was not rooted out for a long time. Indeed, one of the consequences was the emergence of military monastic orders, "warriors who had dedicated their lives and their arms to the service of Christ."[29] According to historians, these orders were suppressed by the pope, not because of their anti-Christian behavior, but because they became too powerful and thereby threatened the power of the bishops and other ecclesiastics.

What can the Crusades tell us about the central problem of this chapter, namely, that the church can become an unconscious victim of its environment and become its champion rather than acting as a leavening and redeeming influence? And if something can be learned, how can the same problem be avoided? Has the Christian church improved from the times of the Crusades? If not, why not?

The Crusades can be approached from a number of sociological perspectives. One would be to evaluate them on the basis of their function for the western society in which they occurred. From this perspective it has been said that the Crusades were the means by which the Christian church was able to produce order out of all the warring factions and religious fractioning that was rampant. Likewise, the Crusades helped the church achieve fuller control, especially by the pope over the European society, and thus preserve the golden age of the *Corpus Christianum* when the church and its political arm jointly ruled over a stable order.

A secular function of the Crusades was to unify various principalities, to force competing kingdoms to cooperate in a common cause, and to establish trade routes and commercial ventures.

But the negative functions (dysfunctions) of the Crusades seem to outweigh the value or desirability of the Crusades. The carnage which resulted from the Crusades, to say nothing of the suffering and deprivation, does not seem to be justified considering what was achieved. The unification of princedoms and kingdoms as a consequence of the Crusades cannot be proved. Nor can the possibility be denied that political unity and harmony, to say nothing of the development of commerce and trade, could have come some other way.

From another perspective, the evolutionary standpoint, the Crusades are a stage in the development of the church from a more primitive and barbaric institution to a more humane and Christian one. But the concept of progress in evolution in general, and of the Christian church in particular, presents some serious problems. If scientists in general hesitate to talk about "progress" in biological evolution, are Christians who look at the church in any better position? Hardly!

It might be remonstrated that the church no longer sends thousands of the faithful on crusades; that it could never do anything so brutal and evil! Nevertheless, in modern times the church has done things which seem not too different. For instance, it has prayed for success of its nation in war, even when the same church was found in two nations at war with each other, as with Lutherans and even Mennonites in World War II. It has also preached that communism must be stopped with all the destructive might at its disposal, and it has condoned the bombing of Japanese cities in which thousands were cremated. The church does not go on crusades anymore; it does its crusading in a more sophisticated way. So evolution is taking place after all in technique and subtlety, but not in basic commitments.

Thus if the evolutionary perspective is used in understanding the church's participation and espousal of the Crusades, it reveals no "progress" but merely a change in the church's development, from more simple to more complex warfare, or from more crude to more sophisticated warfare — but warfare still. Thus the evolutionary perspective is not very fruitful.

Analytical perspectives might seem more helpful. That is, a scientific attempt to understand and describe what the Crusades were might help to understand other crusades and relevant behavior in general. The scientific-analytic perspective can help us understand the causes and the nature of crusades, at least to a limited extent. The social-situational causes for the Crusades have already been mentioned. The analytical aspects of the Crusades still remain to be stated. How did crusades emerge, and what were their constituent elements?

1. They were the expressions of the actions of persons attempting to enhance their social status and power. The pope's power was enhanced by being the leader of the Crusades, as was the power of the princes and knights who led and organized expeditions. The status of the faithful was enhanced by participating in an expedition and distinguishing themselves by some act of piety and heroism.

2. They were the overt outlets for the need to objectify Christian acts of piety in order to assure more assurance of eternal status. This is illustrated in the overall attempt to wrest the Holy Sepulchre and other relics from the hands of the infidel. The establishment of shrines, hostels, and other foundations and communities further illustrates the desire to enhance assurance of spiritual status, to participate in establishing God's rule on earth. Although closely related to the prior point, the desire to preserve the shrines and to spread Christian rule and influence was an aspect of the attempt to spread the kingdom across the face of the earth.

3. They were symbolic expressions of piety, faithfulness, and faith. Faith and piety are expressed by behavior. But some behaviors are more important and significant than others. To pray daily is a symbol of piety, but to free the holy city from infidels is doubly significant. for not only is it an act of piety, but it is also a symbol that the enemies of Christ have been vanquished!

Marching under the sign of the cross in visual form as one expresses his piety is doubly significant. The overt act of piety in freeing a shrine from pagan control combined with the symbolism of a procession under the cross is a powerful phenomenon! Rarely has such a perfect combination been achieved. The only problem with this beautiful combination is that the symbol and the overt act contradict themselves. A more consistent combination of symbol and act would be to march under the symbol of a dish and towel and then literally wash dirty feet and hands in the slums, or to march under a symbol of a cup and then give the unfortunate members of society the chance to drink and eat.

4. A final constituent of the Crusades was the perennial attempt to relate a transcendental entity to mundane existence. Beyond the problem of the concrete expression of faith is the problem of how one makes the connection between the spiritual and the human and relative. What is religion? Is it an attitude or feeling? Is it a creed or recitation of correct dogma? Is it the performance of certain rituals and ceremonies? Is it fellowship with others in a shared faith? Is it a way of life which includes mutual concern for each other's welfare and well-being?

Religion is all of these things, if the analysis of the Christian church's behavior is any indication, although there has rarely if ever been a uniform stress on all of the dimensions at one time. This points to the problem mentioned above: The more the "spiritual" (nonsocial) aspects have been stressed, the more religion has seemed to be irrelevant to society; on the other hand, the more religion has been thought to be social in character, the more "compromising" of Christianity has taken place. The problem of deciding what pure religion was for the Christian church of the Middle Ages was largely decided in favor of both ends of the continuum, but without any attempt to harmonize the two ends. That is, the church of the Crusades correctly decided that Christianity is a spiritual reality *and* a social system, but proceeded to misplace the content of the genuine reality. The spiritual and social nature of Christianity is incontrovertible, but in determining the content of the two realms is where the crusading church went wrong.

Still the question that confronts sociologists is: What is the use of understanding all the facts about the Crusades? The age-old question of "knowledge for what?" confronts us with considerable force. What good would it be for a church to know what causes crusades and how they are constituted, if that church is not able to use the information? What good is it for a church to know about crusades when it is blinded to its own role in causing crusades?

The cynic might say that the church could use the information concerning the nature and causes of crusades in order to plan for bigger and better crusades. But this is hardly an option, since the church in recent years has become even more expert in leading economic, social, and political crusades against blacks and other minority groups. Knowledge about the Crusades is useful only if the knowledge can somehow be utilized to help the church out of its self-deception. The author assumes that the information can be used to become more like what the church was intended to be.

How can a religion which is both transcendental and social at the same time correctly discover the correct interpretation of the content of the religion? Has the Christian church ever fully correctly interpreted what true religion really is?

The answer is negative. The Christian church has been a victim of total ideology to a greater extent than any other human institution, mainly or precisely because its claims are so profoundly sweeping. No nation ever was completely mistaken about objective situation because its intentions were an expression or consequence of that situation itself, whereas Christianity, and other religions for that matter, has professed a transcendental ideal, and has presumed it was achieving it. The fatal and tragic role of religion is to presume to point beyond the objective situation to a higher goal. This, however, creates the possibility of total ideology by the church's becoming victimized by what it rejects. That is, it can be duped into thinking it is achieving its own goals when in reality it is serving the interests and purposes of the historical conditions in which it tries to build its new kingdom. It becomes identified with society. (See option C, page 48.)

The Vision
of a Free Church

All evidence suggests that the Christian church has normally been seduced and captured by the spirit of its age. Rather than speaking out in the prophetic voice, the representative of the transcendent reality, it has been the perpetrator of evils in total contradiction to its purpose and profession. There is nothing very new in this harsh observation, for most people with "singleness of eye" have said the same.

But is there any evidence in history that a segment of Christianity has avoided this deception? Where is the segment of Christianity that has spoken out against the evils of war, poverty, domination, ethnocentrism, secularism, and the dehumanizing aspects of technology and overpopulation? Where is the church that has done something about these issues?

One of the most poignant and powerful judgments of the Christian church to have appeared in recent years is C. Wright Mills' "A Pagan Sermon to the Christian Clergy." This article is written by a nonreligious sociologist, who nevertheless believes that Christianity should be true to itself. In genuine sorrow he says:

> As a social and a personal force, religion has become a dependent variable. It does not originate; it reacts. It does not denounce; it adapts. It does not set forth new models of conduct and sensibility; it imitates. . . . In a quite direct sense, religion has generally become part of the false consciousness of the world and of itself.[1]

A common idea held by many thinkers today is that the only groups which have not been totally seduced by their environment are the sect groups! This is a reversal from several generations ago, when sectarianism was condemned and equated with Satan's domains. Tolstoy maintained that the sect groups were the only Christian groups who were not totally deceived by the material environment and who "saw things as they really were."[2] Though he is speaking specifically to the war issue, J. Milton Yinger makes the following statement, which he applies to other aspects of religion as well:

> The least ambiguous assertion of a universalist ethic (but not necessarily, therefore, the most powerful) in the face of

the divisions of war is found in sectarian pacifism. Here is direct opposition to the policies of government.[3]

In defining universalism in religion, Yinger is not referring to theology. Rather, he is referring to religion which is not bound to a particular time and space. "A religion that is confined to one stable society is an instrument in the pursuit of its individual and group values and a compensation for the failure to achieve them; but it is never a repudiation of these values."[4] Yinger's universal religions, on the other hand, behave differently:

> These religions create tensions with the political order; they encourage loyalties that are larger than the tribe or nation. A unified God for the entire world, particularly a God of love, brings a demand for brotherliness that may sharply contradict the requirements of citizenship.[5]

There are, however, a few groups which have through part of their history protested these evils. In their place they have substituted nonresistance to war. They have practiced equality and brotherhood, in some places sharing goods in a communal sort of way. And they have undermined the concept of domination by considering all alike in the fellowship so that they have not distinguished between laity and clergy, wealthy and poor, strong and weak. Instead, they have practiced mutual aid and consensual decision-making. Furthermore, these groups have maintained a rigorous resistance to the wholesale adoption of technology as an inherent aspect of the good life, and have followed, rather, Christ's dictum that "man's life does not consist of the abundance of the things he possesses." In their concern for human values, some of these groups have stressed rural life because it better fosters healthful human relations.

The following section will attempt to describe objectively a group that has tried to remain unseduced on some of the critical issues alluded to previously, and hence has been a "free church" in the sense which will be defined later. The evidence must speak for itself, however; the reader is invited to examine critically the evidence presented here to test whether the author himself is not a victim of total ideology.

War

Since its origin in the Reformation, the authentic stream of the Anabaptist Church has consistently rejected participation in war in any form. As one statement puts it, "we can have no part in carnal warfare or conflict between nations, nor in strife between classes, groups, or individuals . . . and must consider members who violate these principles as transgressors and out of fellowship with the church."[6] That not all Mennonites have held to this position need not be argued here. The fact is that this position has been held to for over 400 years, and adhered to in practice throughout this time by a substantial segment of the Mennonite Church.

The refusal to participate in war has taken numerous forms but they have all been derived from the refusal to substitute the "way of the cross" for a "marching under the cross" as evidenced in the Crusades. The theological base for this position cannot be argued here; there are numerous adequate treatments available. The important factor in this discussion is that a group has maintained that war in any manner or form is contrary to the will of God and the Christian faith, and has proceeded to live according to this conviction. Such refusal to take up arms is not limited to Anabaptists alone. At least three groups are known as the "historic peace churches."[7]

This refusal has meant persecution, exile, imprisonment, forced enlistment in military institutions, and even executions. It has involved emigrations and establishment of colonies in countries which do not demand conscription, as, for example, the migration of Mennonites from Prussia to Russia in search of exemption from military service. It has involved various forms of testimony to government and the public regarding the church's position on war, in an attempt to achieve exemption for its own members, but also to witness to the members of society at large.

The rejection of war has also been connected with other positions which can only be mentioned, but which are significant for our case. The first and most important is the rejection of giving one's ultimate loyalty to the state. Rather, the Mennonites have said, their loyalty belongs first and foremost to the church of Christ. "Association with the state was at best sub-Christian, whereas the church represented the kingdom of God."[8] The rejection of the state as the sovereign institution has included also the rejection of holding office, and of participation in high level political processes.

Poverty and Wealth

Christ made some startlingly stringent demands regarding His followers and wealth. "It is easier," He said, "for a camel to go through a needle's eye, than for a rich man to enter into the kingdom of God" (Luke 18:25). He also said, "sell all that thou hast, and distribute unto the poor, and thou shalt have treasure in heaven" (Luke 18:22).

The Mennonite movement has historically been very skeptical of wealth and has stressed the importance of mutual aid and communal living in varying degrees. The Anabaptists following Peter Ridemann and Jacob Hutter held to the significance of mutuality in wealth and material goods to such absolutes that they decided to have "all things in common." This offshoot of Anabaptism is world-renowned for its concern about the well-being of its members.[9] Granted that the sharing is limited to members of the Hutterite colonies, it is a condition that they have coveted for all men. The Hutterites seriously believe that the communal life is God's way for all men, and expect all men ultimately to see it their way.

Other groups within the Mennonite Church have practiced varying degrees of communal living, such as the Old Colony Mennonites, who exemplify a semi-communal system since the church holds official title to all lands and controls how the land is divided and used. Other things that are communally owned include the pasture lands, schools, and church buildings. They practice considerable mutual aid in the form of mutual aid insurance for fires and other catastrophes. The more impoverished and handicapped among them are supplied by voluntary contributions.[10] Other more contemporary Mennonite groups such as the Reba Place Fellowship in Evanston, Illinois, are recapturing this concern for poverty and mutuality. The

73

Evanston group is a communal group which attempts to transplant the ideal to urban settings. [11]

Since Mennonites reject the state as the handmaiden of the kingdom, they have themselves implemented their concern about poverty and degradation through the establishment of relief and service programs to the remote corners of the world. The Mennonite Central Committee, in existence since 1920, has distributed food and clothing in almost every country ravaged by war, famine, or destruction. A multimillion annual budget is currently raised among Mennonites to help the unfortunate around the world. The extent and forms that their concern for the poor of the earth has taken can only be alluded to. Voluntary sharing of goods with friend and foe, sending of supplies to foreign sufferers, and establishment of rehabilitation units are only three examples. One contemporary example which is achieving considerable publicity and appreciation is the Mennonite Disaster Service, an organization that sends able-bodied men into a disaster area such as tornado or flood and gives assistance of all kinds to the victims, all at no cost, "in the name of Christ."

Domination

Mennonites have taken seriously the dictum of Christ that he who would follow Him should "deny himself, and take up his cross, and follow me" (Matthew 16:24). Their rejection of domination is integrally related to their concept of nonresistance and rejection of loyalty to the state. Both inherently assume the necessity of domination. Mennonites believe that "my kingdom is not of this world."

Thus, the concept of brotherhood has been deeply engrained in the Mennonite Church. In fact, Troeltsch defines the Mennonite Church in essence as constituting a brotherhood where membership in the fellowship is determined by a common commitment without any status distinctions except that of charismatic gifts. [12] Membership in the brotherhood involves relinquishment of worldly status symbols and the disregarding of status distinctions themselves, so that the clergy-laity distinction, for example, is denied. Further, it involves the concept of mutual support, caring and sharing, where the welfare of the neighbor is as important as one's own; hence, the importance of the Sermon on the Mount, where mutual concern is given absolute significance.

One of the most exciting historical evidences of the refusal to dominate other human beings is the adamant refusal to keep slaves in America. Mennonites migrated to America in 1663, and as early as 1693 issued a joint statement with the Quakers at Germantown protesting slavery and urging all Mennonites to testify against slavery. Thus in league with the Quakers, with whom this statement is connected, they promulgated the first-known statement against the sin of owning slaves. What is more, in contrast to the Quakers, there is no known case of a Mennonite owning slaves. In fact, many are known to have participated in the freeing of slaves when they lived in an area conducive to this kind of activity, as in Virginia.[13]

This position has been further borne out historically in the Mennonite tradition in numerous ways. One is the refusal to hold office in any state function, since this involves "lording it over them" in a fashion not in keeping with the Christian faith. In the economic realm, Mennonites have never fared very well in business and industry, again at least partially because this involves domination over others, which does not square with their gospel. In general, where Mennonites have been in employer positions, they have practiced an egalitarianism toward labor far ahead of organized labor demands.

Ethnocentrism and Nationalism

As indicated above, Mennonites have historically been so negatively disposed toward domination that they have bent over backward not to become involved in any "lording" functions that might dominate others in any way. Ethnocentrism is a closely related concept, especially when it is identified with the state. But it is still possible for a group to be so ethnocentric that it considers itself infinitely superior and unconcerned about the rest of the world.

Again, it is now alleged by many outsiders that the Anabaptists were probably the leading missionaries of the Reformation period. In fact, it has been proposed that Mennonites launched the modern missionary movement:

> The gathering of small congregations by believers' baptism went on apace, and Anabaptism spread in many areas closed to the state churches by their acceptance of the principle of territorialism. The Anabaptists represent thereby an early Protestant vision of a world mission unrestricted by territorial limitations, and in a unique fashion foreshadow the later concept of the church as a community of missionary people. [14]

Anabaptists were missionaries in a certain sense by default, for in their enthusiasm for the new life they had found they were persecuted and expelled from many countries. In the process they came into contact with many persons in many lands, establishing churches where they went. By the end of the sixteenth century, Anabaptism was found in most of the countries on the European continent.

But Anabaptism did not remain free of ethnocentrism. Largely because of persecution the Anabaptists began to "keep to themselves," and developed communities of the faithful, sealed off from the rest of the world in close-knit colonies in Prussia, Russia, Canada, the United States, and elsewhere, This period of withdrawal served to develop unique cultural social forms to the extent that in many communities missionary work was out of the question, if for no other reason than that conversion meant the adoption of another culture, which many potential converts could not accept. More will be said on this later. In any case it must be admitted that in many Mennonite communities a feeling of being better Christians than non-Mennonites has been rather pervasive. [15]

Mennonite nationalism was practically nonexistent for at least two hundred years. For as previously indicated, the state was not part of life within the kingdom of God. However, as Mennonites began to be accepted as a legitimate sect, as for example, the Dutch were in 1672, "to be protected in the free exercise of their religion," many segments began to identify the purpose of the kingdom of God with that of the state. By World War II, in the United States, for example, up to one half of the young men in some Mennonite groups participated in the military actions. In some other countries, such as Germany, the Mennonites participated extensively in the war effort.

Secularism

Rarely have Mennonites been accused of secularism! On the contrary, many people outside as well as inside the movement have categorized the Mennonites as being irrelevant because of their attempts to make all of life sacred, as though they thought they were already living in the kingdom of God. And it is precisely this commandment to live in the kingdom of God that forced upon them the dualistic, "two-kingdom ethic."

The Mennonites have historically believed that they were called to live and work in the kingdom of God.

> . . . the Brethren were attempting the existential realization of the commands of Christ, fully aware that man is at all times a citizen of two worlds, and consequently that he has to make a decision for the one or the other. The Scriptures, mainly the New Testament, were for them the great textbook of the kingdom of God, understood in the twofold meaning of the kingdom — the one that has already come and "is among us," and the one which is still to come. From the Scriptures they learned also the need for an incessant fight against the Prince of Darkness to whom one must not yield even on a small scale. This stark biblical dualism shines out in many an Anabaptist tract.[16]

The conviction that every decision must be made in the context of life in the kingdom of God can easily be taken as a definition of sacralization, or the opposite of secularism. The Mennonite tradition has struggled to keep this concept of the life in the kingdom of God alive, although it has fallen into the trap of legalism so often and so seriously that the Mennonite tradition has often been dismissed as idealistic groups unworthy of serious attention.[17]

In any case, the priorities seemed clear in Mennonite history. The important values were not progress in the scientific and technological and economic realms, but rather in the realms of stressing the inner life of the congregation, the importance of self-denial and *following Jesus*. Dietrich Bonhoeffer popularized this concept during World War II, but he rightfully rebukes the Lutheran churches of cheap grace and refers to the Mennonites as having embraced this integral part of the gospel.[18]

The sacralization of life in the kingdom of God implies a stress on ethical behavior, both inside the congregation and in the "world." Strict discipline and mutual admonition are practiced. Thus the avoidance of worldliness, as they see it, involves refusal to participate in worldly "fads" and other activities which reflect lust, pride, and self-enhancement and worship. The Amish segment of the Mennonite Church evidences this trait to its most absurd extreme. This attempt to keep everything within the realm of the sacred has backfired in a tragic manner.[19]

Population Explosion and Technology

The relation of these two problems to the Mennonite tradition appears rather farfetched. But there is a connection. Mennonites have traditionally been rural, and their rural life has contained an answer to the consequences of population density and technology — namely, alienation. The Mennonite community is a remarkable "commonwealth," a fact which has been documented numerous times. Although the cause for its stress on rural living may have been accidental (the Anabaptists emerged in a more urban context), it was soon accepted as a reflection of the authentic life implied in the kingdom of God as pictured in the Scriptures.

In the rural Mennonite community each individual is allowed to become an individual, unique, with a character and personality that is part of the larger whole. Among the Old Colony Mennonites, the place of each individual in the social system is assured, regardless of how "square" or odd he is.[20] He is accepted into the circle — in fact, consists in it without any other criterion of evaluation. As a matter of fact, in many Mennonite communities, an individual is designated not by his given name, or even surname, but by a trait which describes his uniqueness and marks him in some functional as well as status way as part of the ongoing community. Hence

78

the term "one-armed Dyck" refers to the fact that this certain man had lost an arm in an accident. One of the author's grandfathers was known as Bonesetter Wall, which indicated his functional role in the community, beyond the fact that by status he was also a preacher.

Technology has always been avoided as much as possible by Mennonites because they always suspected that too much "modernity" would allow alienation to enter between individuals and the original idea of brotherhood would be stifled or weakened. The Old Colony has long tried to keep automobiles and electric lights from its members because of what this might do to relationships between church members. The *Gemeinschaft* character of a community is quickly lost with the introduction of very much technology, as the Old Colony illustrates. The Hutterites, who have been most successful in controlling the use of technology, have adopted only as much as they feel they can safely handle without disrupting their life in the community. Most observers would agree that they have solved the problem fairly well.

The Mennonite community is fast becoming a museum piece of the past. There is increasing alienation even among Mennonites themselves, but this does not deny that there were basic issues to which these communities have been speaking. Community champions such as Baker Brownell and A. E. Morgan cannot praise these communities enough. It is highly probable that alienation has been avoided in these communities more so than in other more urban and technical environments. But the bald fact is that urbanization, the consequence of population increase and technology, is rapidly imposing itself on all, including Mennonites, who are finding it hard to make the transition and retain any semblance of community.

An interesting side light on the population issue is that the decline in birth rate in one Mennonite group has preceded the declining birth rate of the general American population. The Mennonite decline began in 1952, at least five years before the general decline began — this in spite of the fact that Mennonites are still predominantly a rural people. It is tempting to hypothesize that this reduction is a result of growing alienation produced by increasing population pressure and technology, but evidence to substantiate the thesis is nonexistent.

Is there any evidence in history to indicate that a Christian group had avoided the deception of becoming a reflection of the "spirit of the age"? The Mennonite Church tradition has been briefly cited as an illustration that groups can be found who have refused to be the mirror image of the society in which they have found themselves. Other groups have in some manner protested the secular age and pointed to a new age that has not yet come. No other group has been as broad in its rejection of the mundane aspects of society as have the Mennonites, without being subject to the accusation of asceticism.

A few questions need reviewing. 1. Why did this unusual movement emerge? 2. Why are these groups not more widely known? In fact, why have these groups been despised and rejected? Why were the Mennonites, Quakers, Brethren, and other groups considered *Ketzer* and anarchists, undesirables? 3. Why has the Mennonite position not been more widely adopted? An answer to these questions is a most interesting case of an ideology within an ideology.

That the non-Christian — be he an official of the state, or a wealthy landowner, or a person bent on self-serving pleasure — would not be very much attracted to an austere faith such as this one is understandable. But the rejection by other Christians of the Mennonite kind of interpretation of the Christian gospel has more interest for us. A far more serious fact is the "mainline Protestant" rejection of the teachings and behaviors promulgated by many if not most of the "sectarian" groups beginning with the Albigensians and Waldensians in the twelfth century.

One interpretation lies in the church and sect typology based on the sociologists' concept of stratification and power: That church organization which had the socio-economic power on its side was able to subordinate all other competing or threatening movements or to have them exterminated. Very often the superior power was gained by alliance with the state in some form, as with the Catholic Church in Spain for many centuries and the Zwinglian Church in Switzerland during the early Reformation, to mention only two instances.

But the power theory does not exhaust all the possible reasons for the rejection by Christendom of the absolutist positions on the Gospels taken by the sect groups. Another could be the unwillingness to admit the correctness of the sectarian position, for example, on the absolute evil nature of war. For upon admission of such a fact, the church would have to lose its prestigious position and become an exile church. Thus, it is possible that the church has made a very calculated choice against the sectarian positions because it feels that the loss of leadership and influence in the world would be greater than the influence gained by the world-rejecting stance. This is well stated by J. Milton Yinger:

> Freedom from the structures of power raised the question of powerlessness. "The dilemma of the churches" is clear at this point, for to claim separation from the state is to reduce one's ability to influence the decisions of the state; while institutional union raises the likelihood that a church which seems to have a voice in political decisions is actually only an echo of decisions made on political grounds.[21]

The reason, therefore, that many Christian denominations and groups have rejected the radical discipleship approach to the Christian faith may be simply that they have decided that the liabilities outweigh the assets, for what would the world look like if the church voluntarily gave it over to the pagans! They would admit that there have been some compromises and loss of faithfulness to the gospel, but that that is worth the risk of invoking God's displeasure:

> How to be simultaneously in politics (and thus to influence it) and beyond politics (thus to challenge it) is an ancient problem among the religions. . . . It is perhaps the recognition of this dilemma that has been partly responsible for the recent reduction on the sharpness of separation of churches and state in the United States.[22]

81

The universal character of religious truth suggests the third and possibly most significant reason why so few religious groups have given radical obedience to the "universal character of religious truth." It is simply that a predominant segment of the Christian church has never been able to see the options open to it, being blinded by the conditions of existence. How else can one explain the Christian church's belief in and support of the morality and utility of war, and the necessity of domination within the church through hierarchy and outside the church through concurring with the practices of stratification or domination prevalent in society?

According to sociologists, the only way that a member of society can go free from a total ethnocentric "tribal bias" is to belong to a social system or reference group that transcends the tribal or national boundary. Therefore the only way for the Christian church to be able to be conscious of its own captivity by the values and norms of the specific society in which it finds itself is to belong to a universal or supranational society or nation. This has been well stated by J. Milton Yinger:

> We shall hold that the development of religions that seem to transcend the social systems from which they come is the result of creative religious leaders, struggling with the problems with which religion is basically concerned. Social change and culture contact have made them discontented with the traditional solutions. . . . These religions create tensions with the political order; they encourage loyalties that are larger than the tribe or nation. A united God for the entire world, particularly a God of love, brings a demand for brotherliness that may sharply contradict the requirements of citizenship. . . . A religion that is confined to one stable society is an instrument in the pursuit of its individual and group values and a compensation for the failure to achieve them but it is a repudiation of these values.[23]

This universal loyalty and identity can be spoken of and referred to in many ways, but the most common is the image of the kingdom of God, the kingdom that is already here but is yet to come. This citizenship in a nation that is here, yet still in the future, to be ruled by God Himself, determines the entire stance of the Christian. His norms, goals, and belief are informed by this vision that is described in many ways in the Bible. This eschatological stance has characterized almost all religious utopian and sectarian groups.

It is this very "other citizenship" which has enabled these adherents to "see things as they really are" in the secular realm in which they reluctantly must still make their abode. The glamour and show of the "world" has no ultimate seductive power to them, for they are going toward a city whose "builder and maker is God." In the conflict between Zwingli and the early Anabaptist leaders, the critical issue was the basis from which the argument was conducted: that of the defense of the status quo, or at least taking its cues from it; or the reference to a new ethic, completely unrelated to the former.

The essence of the free church is therefore the awareness of the possibility that the mind can be "darkened" by the most subtle and dangerous temptation of all — that of being unable to see the truth because of a total involvement in the temporary order, which by definition, is not objective. The traditional definition of the free church, which refers to its separation from the state and other institutions such as the economic, is thus only the preliminary approach to the central issue of being free to hear the voice of God and obey it because there are no other loyalties which seduce and prostitute the perception and cognition of reality. A free church is that group which lives by the universal character of the Christian gospel, in which nation, clan, class, creed, or institution is almost totally irrelevant, or if meaningful, subordinated to the higher cause in order to realize the kingdom of God.

This universal character of truth has a noble history. The political men revered in history are those who saw the world as a community, rather than from their own cave. Dag Hammarskjöld is remembered because of his dedication to the common brotherhood of all men. Since this is all the more true when held in Christian perspective, the great prostitution of the Christian church has been her yielding to the worship

83

of a particular God who loved a particular people — for example, the Americans. The New Testament speaks loudly and clearly about the universality and nonparticularity of the Christian faith; there is no male nor female, bond nor free, Jew or Scythian, but all are children of the heavenly Father.

The free church is therefore that church which is aware of the ease with which man's perceptions and cognitive faculties become conditioned to and by the temporal order, and which is suspicious of every pronouncement that does not have an objective basis in transcendental truth. It is that church which has been aware of the insights popularized by Hegel, Marx, Freud, and Mannheim, even though they lived long before these men wrote. It is the knowledge that man is self-centered, that he sees things in his own interest, and that he can be totally and unintentionally unaware of his own motivations and desires.

The free church does not merely resist control by the state, nor does it resist merely coercion by the state or by other social institutions. Furthermore, it does not merely resist the compulsion and coercion of folk and culture religion, such as the Faith in Faith prevalent in America. It rejects all of these influences and could be considered a free church on this count alone; but the free church is free of coercion by the conditioned nature of human perception and cognition as expressed in the particularism of tribe, clan, state, and nation.

The free church member is first of all a member of the kingdom of God, a member of the body of Christ, that universal collectivity which has been commissioned by Christ to "prepare the way of the Lord." He is next a member of a temporal and spatical localization of the body. Then he is a member of the brotherhood of mankind, and only tentatively a member of a nation-state.

In conclusion, a few sociological principles can be illustrated:

1. The ethnocentricism principle. Man defends, boosts, and is identified with the group to which he belongs. If his primary membership is in a labor union, he sees everything from that perspective. If he is foremost an American, he sees the world

from that perspective. But if he is first a member of the kingdom of God, he sees lesser loyalties in their proper perspective.

2. The socialization principle. Man normally becomes like the other men in the social system in which he lives and moves. The reference group of the individual or group determines the nature of values, beliefs, and norms that the individual or group internalizes. If man is born and reared in the family of the kingdom of God, his attitudes, values, and goals will reflect it.

3. The reciprocity principle. Man does not ordinarily give something away without getting something in equal value in return. Thus he will not give up power and status unless he receives something in trade. Unfortunately there is little that takes the place of power, status, and prestige, and therefore few will voluntarily give them up — Christians throughout history included. The only way reciprocity can be broken is through the concept of deferred or sublimated exchange — receiving future payment or receiving payment in different currency. This different currency is the reward of pleasing the Lord of history, and the pleasure of support and respect from other peers in the "colony of heaven."

4. The self-deceiving principle. Man has an uncanny ability to misinterpret and pervert objective reality. Thus an old adage has stood the test of time: "Things perceived to be real are real in their consequences." This principle holds along the entire gamut, from the paranoid who believes he is being hunted and therefore is able to interpret all of objective reality to prove his point, to the nation which can convince its population that communism is the menace which must be stopped if man is to survive. This deception is especially glaring in the context of the possession of atomic weapons by the leading world powers. In a very significant volume which carefully analyzes and reviews all of the scientifically verifiable researchers on human social behavior, Berelson and Steiner concluded with these somber words:

> Perhaps the character of behavioral science man can best be grasped through his orientation to reality. . . . First, he

is extremely good at adaptive behavior — at doing or learning to do things that increase his chances for survival or for satisfaction . . . (but) in his quest for satisfaction, man is not just a seeker of truth, but of deceptions, of himself as well as others. When man can come to grips with his needs by actually changing the environment, he does so. But when he cannot achieve such "realistic" satisfaction, he tends to take the other path; to modify what he sees to be the case, what he thinks he wants, and what he thinks others want. . . . For the truth is, apparently, that no matter how successful man becomes in dealing with his problems, he still finds it hard to live in the real world undiluted.[24]

Hardly anything more eloquent could be said of the human condition.

In light of these conclusions, the free church concept is truly audacious, for it actually proposes that groups in history have been able to be cognitively free. The Mennonites are an illustration of a group which has at least partially succeeded in this stride to be free. The principles that Mennonites have stood for are freedom from coercion by the state and nation and from social and psychological forces. An unmitigated insistence on this proposition, however, would itself illustrate a cognitive seduction and conditioning on the part of the author. The important next step in the development of the argument is to take a closer look at Anabaptist origins and history, seeing at first hand what happened, how it happened, and thus how the argument presented so far can be substantiated. The critical stance of the reader is thus imperative for the corroboration or rejection of the central arguments of this book.

The Dynamics of Protest of Total Ideology

In one of his memorable statements, Walter Rauschenbusch says, "The philosophy regnant in any age is always the direct outgrowth of the sum total of life in the age."[1] Explaining his premise further, he says, "Every human institution creates a philosophy which hallows it to those who profit by it and allays the objections of those who are victimized by it."[2] Rauschenbusch, who does not exclude the church from this formula, spends a great deal of his energy trying to urge the church to recover its true heritage as he sees it. Although he may be only partially right in what he sees as the role of the church in society, his basic premise cannot be challenged.

If this is true, then churches and religious groups of various kinds are potentially the victim of total ideology, as are other institutions in society. It is possible, however, that a religious grouping is as likely to free itself from total ideology as any other group — more likely, in fact, if the transcendental aspect of Christianity is assumed. And as this chapter suggests, it is possible for a religious group to emerge which will recognize and protest total ideology. It will also illustrate briefly how this happened, describe the dynamics of the process, and finally analyze the cause-effect relationships, insofar as this is possible within the limits of the space available.

In recent times, man has become increasingly aware of the sources of his own thought patterns and thought content. Nietzsche, about a century ago, "had set down a host of aphorisms on the ways in which needs determined the perspectives through which we interpret the world so that even sense perceptions are permeated with value-preferences."[3] Before Nietzsche, Marx had written about the economically determined bases of thought, suggesting that people were limited and informed by the economic conditions in which they lived. And of course Freud and his followers later proceeded to lay bare the subjectivity of human behavior and ratiocination.

It is impossible to treat adequately the development and nature of the discovery that our thought forms and processes are conditioned and determined by the nature of the social conditions in which we live. Suffice it to say that the "sociology of knowledge came into being with the signal hypothesis that even truths were to be held socially accountable, were to be related to the historical society in which they emerged."[4] The import of this hypothesis is that truth, no matter what type of truth, scientific or even theological, could be derived from and predicted by the conditions of the society in which it emerged. This discovery has set in motion forces which have revolutionized the intellectual tradition of the West, if not also the East.

One consequence of this intellectual revolution has been the analysis of western history in the light of the sociology of knowledge. Thus history has become no longer the study of objective events, but the analysis of underlying causes, and "second-guessing" the perpetrators of those events themselves. One of the important thinkers who followed this procedure was Karl Mannheim, whose premises are described in the following statement:

> Social position determines the "perspective, i.e., the manner in which one views an object, what one perceives in it, and how one construes it in his thinking." The situational determination of thought does not render it invalid; it does, however, particularize the scope of the inquiry and the limits of its validity.[5]

On this premise, Mannheim proceeds to analyze the basic categories of western societal structure.

According to Mannheim, a major watershed in the history of western civilization was the breakdown of the medieval society dominated by the church. The emergence of pluralistic thought patterns and social structures changed completely the concepts of thought, authority, social organization, and religion. "It is with this clashing of modes of thought, each of which has the same claims to representational validity, that for the first time there is rendered possible the emergence of the question which is so fateful, but also so fundamental in the history of thought, namely, how it is possible that identical human thought processes concerned with the same world produce divergent conceptions of the world."[6]

By the highwater mark of the Reformation, there had

developed many "divergent conceptions of the world." Although most were religious, and had already begun to emerge as far back as the twelfth century, some of the most significant were the Peasants' Revolt and the Muenster Rebellion. Many historians of the Reformation link the Anabaptists with Müntzer and the Peasants' Revolt, as did Luther and other Reformation leaders themselves. However, convincing evidence now suggests that the "mainline" Anabaptists were not as "chiliastic" as they were reputed to be. Objective commentators suggest that one major trait that contributed to the Anabaptist "divergent conception" was their repudiation of the state church. "The Anabaptists would have nothing to do with a state church; and this was the main point in their separation from the Lutherans, Zwinglians, and Calvinists. It was perhaps the one conception on which parties among them were in absolute accord. The real church, which might be small or great, was for them an association of believing people. . . . "[7]

Similarly, Thomas G. Sanders suggests that the Anabaptists looked upon the *Volkskirche* "as no church at all."[8] Sanders maintains that the Anabaptists defined Christianity in a way totally different from all other conceptions. "Therefore, he who truly considered himself a Christian abjured his association with the politically sponsored *Volkskirche* and joined the community of those whose religious experience denoted their conversion."[9] The following quote best sums up what seems to be an accepted interpretation of Anabaptist concern:

> The Anabaptists, by holding that the real church was constituted by a separated group who, upon repentance, justification, and regeneration, underwent a genuine baptism for the first time, made quite clear that they did not consider the members of the state church real Christians. Association with the state was at best sub-Christian, whereas the church represented the kingdom of God. . . . In sectarian fashion, they saw the church as a voluntary, internally organized group, in which all members, equally Christian, determined the nature of Christian thought and life. . . . "[10]

Thus, the rejection of a *Volkskirche* was the Anabaptist

"trademark," which, however, had numerous ancillary concepts such as nonresistance, nonswearing of oaths, and other traits. The consequent behavior of the Anabaptists gives empirical support to the contention that rejection of the *Volkskirche* was the central dynamic. Their consequent refusal to submit themselves to membership in the Zwinglian church, their refusal to defend themselves against harassment by the authorities, their acceptance of martyrdom rather than recantation, their adamant rebaptizing of *Volkskirchliche*, thereby introduced a new and explosive "pluralism" into social thought. The Anabaptists apparently were unable to hold to this position, for Walter Rauschenbusch states:

> The Peasants' Rising in 1525 in Germany embodied the social ideals of the common people; the Anabaptist movement, which began simultaneously, expressed their religious aspirations; both were essentially noble and just; yet both were quenched in streams of blood and have had to wait till our own day for their resurrection in new form.[11]

Another historical account describes the consequent development as follows:

> Anabaptists continued to be divided. The Mennonites were the most numerous, but even they were not bound together in a single fellowship and differed among themselves. . . . Driven by persecution and refusing to resist by force of arms, the Mennonites scattered widely. In the seventeenth century many of the Swiss Mennonites, constrained by persecution, especially in Bern and Zurich, found homes in the Palatinate. Late in the eighteenth century under the religious Catherine the Great many of them moved to South Russia, attracted by the promise of free land and exemption from taxation for a period of years. Numbers were also to make their homes in North and South America, especially the United States.[12]

The rejection of the state church, and the society of the *Corpus Christianum*, introduced into the structure of social thought a new pluralism, one which Mannheim believed to be the first serious challenge to an accepted and coherent social perspective. Although this process had been developing for some time before, Mannheim contends that the coming of the Renaissance and the Reformation accelerated the breakup of a unified society. Whereas the earlier society had been characterized by a monopoly of authority and intellectual thought patterns, the emergence of conflicting authorities, belief systems intellectual apparatuses, and status systems created not only confusion, but also world views which conflicted with each other and which tended toward the "breakdown of the unitary world view."[13]

> The decisive turning-point in modern history was, from the point of view of our problem, the moment in which "Chiliasm" joined forces with the active demands of the oppressed strata of society. The very idea of the dawn of a millennial kingdom on earth always contained a revolutionizing tendency, and the church made every effort to paralyze the situationally transcendent idea with all the means at its command.[14]

It was this incipient "pluralism" which made the emergence of groups like the Anabaptists possible. Mannheim rightly states that in a society in which there is a stable and unitary social system there is no chance for a "divergent view" to emerge. But this does not indicate why the Anabaptists emerged to take the particular position they did. For this we must resort to another thesis which Mannheim proposes, namely, the group source of thought.

> Thus, it is not men in general who think, or even isolated individuals who do the thinking, but men in certain groups who have developed a particular style of thought in an endless series of responses to certain typical situations characterizing their common position.[15]

If we accept Mannheim's proposition, then the Anabaptists developed a common "divergent view" on the basis of an evolution of a common world view based on common experiences. The Anabaptists protested the *Corpus Christianum* because they developed a divergent view on the basis of common experience which conflicted with the existing one.

The common experience would certainly include the almost obsessive reading of the Scriptures, which enabled them to perceive the possibility of a "total ideology" on the part of the state church. Other common experiences included the observations of the corruption of the ecclesiastical system, the hypocrisy and cynicism of the men in positions of holy office, and the exploitation of the masses economically, religiously, and socially. The resentment resulting from observing these abuses was the basic animus that initiated the Anabaptist protest, for Mannheim states that the observer "who has not also discovered the fruitful aspects of resentment in his own experience, will never be in a position to see the phase of Christian ethics described above, to say nothing of being able to understand it."[16]

The rejection of one world view as totally corrupt also demands the development and substitution of another world view. Where did the Anabaptists get theirs and how did it emerge? Only the rudimentary aspects of this can be discussed here. Upon observing how the Reformation leaders equivocated at every turn, the Anabaptists finally must have decided that there was something "fishy" going on. In the long-drawn-out struggle in Zurich between Zwingli and his followers and the Anabaptists, the issue finally got down to the problem of total ideology. The Anabaptists' final point of contention with Zwingli was the role of the state authorities in the establishment of the Reformation.

The Zwinglian leaders maintained that the state authorities needed to be consulted in the process of reforming the Roman Catholic Church, whereas the Anabaptists maintained that only the Scriptures and the Spirit of God should be followed.[17] There was full agreement on what was to be done, but the method was the contention. On the specific point of the mass, which precipitated the break, Zwingli agreed that the mass should be discarded, but he maintained that "the Mass would be discarded as soon as the Council gave orders to this effect."[18]

To this the Anabaptists responded with indignation: "Master Ulrich, you have not the right to leave the decision of this question to the Council. The matter is already decided; the Spirit of God decides it."[19] The Anabaptists were finally discovering what Mannheim says was here discovered for the first time: the socially situated roots of thought and ratiocination.

The discovery of the social-situational roots of thought at first, therefore, took the form of unmasking. In addition to the gradual dissolution of the unitary objective world-view, which to the simple man in the street took the form of a plurality of divergent conceptions of the world, and to the intellectuals presented itself as the irreconcilable plurality of thought styles, there entered into the public mind the tendency to unmask the unconscious situational motivations in group thinking. . . . The concept "ideology" reflects the one discovery which emerged from political conflict, namely, that ruling groups can in their thinking become so intensively interest-bound to a situation that they are simply no longer able to see certain facts which would undermine their sense of domination.[20]

It seems apparent that the critical matter for the early Anabaptists, and the reason which explains their separation from the Zwingli group, was the slowly emerging insight that Zwingli was not aware that he was the victim of social-situational conditioning of thought. The only way that Zwingli's changing positions and repudiations of earlier positions could be explained was that he was the victim of a "total ideology" in which the person or group's total *Weltanschauung* is faulty and is the result of "the collective life of which he partakes."[21] In the Anabaptists' language, he was not willing to submit "to God in the things which the Spirit of God teaches and commands."[22]

What was impossible for the Anabaptists to understand was Zwingli's apparent agreement with the Anabaptists on the biblical validity of their common reforms, but his hesitancy to go along with them in their implementation. The Anabaptists discovered that the Reformation leaders were "beholden" to the civil authorities and thus unable to transcent their social situation, or even worse, could not see the objective reality because of their own involvement in it. It became clear to the Anabaptists that Zwingli felt more secure with the support of the state behind him than in striking out "by faith alone." Hence Anabaptists interpreted reliance on power and position as the reformers' reluctance to give up the power and position which these men held in their reforming role.

The Anabaptists, on the other hand, assumed that if a man knew what was right he would do it "if he was truly free," regardless of the consequences. The Anabaptist denunciation of the reformers as unfaithful must therefore be seen in this light: the Reformation leaders were not faithful to the gospel as the Anabaptist saw it, for they considered success as one of the bases of action. Since the Anabaptists were willing to forsake all and follow Christ's demands literally regardless of what the implications might be, they assumed they were free to see the issues correctly and clearly; anyone who could not see it their way must obviously have hidden motives or perceptions which hindered him from seeing it their way. Hence Zwingli and followers were simply stubborn and rebelling against the will and word of God.

It is impossible to say whether the Anabaptists verbalized or conceptualized in any way the concept of total ideology, but the consequences were nevertheless the same. The Anabaptists held out for a noncompromised loyalty to the kingdom of God and thus rejected Zwingli as a pagan. The Anabaptists reluctantly concluded that Zwingli was not able to make the complete break with the social situation of which he was a part. "The cause of the failure is the compromising attitude (on the part of the preachers), the setting aside the divine Word and adulterating it with the human word."[23]

In commenting on the bases for the break with Zwingli, Conrad Grebel stated, "When we ourselves took to hand the Scriptures, and studied them with reference to various articles, we were in a measure instructed and were led to recognize the existing lack."[24] Stated in a different way, the Anabaptists must have felt that a person who is absolutely objective would come up with the true concept of the kingdom of God upon reading the Bible. The Anabaptists strove to come up with the concept of the kingdom of God as the basic world view by the process of being free from the "total ideology" to which Zwingli was still captive.

The points of contention with Zwingli — which included baptism, nonresistance, the swearing of oaths, and the repudiation of state interference in determining the form and functions of the church — all emerged from a single reference to the claims of the Spirit and Word of God. Whenever an argument or disputation developed, Anabaptists referred to what the Word of God or the Spirit of God said, in contrast to Zwingli, who constantly based his arguments on the temporizing facts of authority, order, and possibility. A historian whom Horsch quotes states the matter succinctly:

> As correct as was Zwingli's general attitude from the viewpoint of the state (sic!) and as great as were the political advantages it secured for his ecclesiastical work, just so inconsistent was it, on the other hand, considered from the evangelical angle, and so sure was it to lead to religious dissensions and conflicts within the Reformation movement. [25]

The Anabaptists promulgated a world view which they felt was a "given" one; one that was "handed down" from "Mount Sinai" without any "political" considerations.

Thus the Anabaptists came up with the particular *Weltanschauung* of the kingdom of God because they in an unconditioned way refused to become victims of a "total ideology." They remained true to the "pure gospel" and hence have been termed "biblicists" and "legalists" with some justification. Stated from the perspective of the sociology of knowledge, it could be said that they remained free from total ideology and accepted a *Weltanschauung* which often has been totally irrelevant to the social conditions of the time. But this is precisely what would be expected! The more "relevant" a group is (and as Zwingli was), the more it is apt to be victim of a "total ideology" and be compromised in the morass of subjective swamps.

A final dimension of the problem is the manner in which the Anabaptists undertook to reform the church. "The Protestant movement set up in the place of revealed salvation, guaranteed by the objective institution of the church, the notion of the subjective certainty of salvation." [26] Whereas the Protestant view resulted from a spiritualizing, individualizing, and subjectivizing system, the Anabaptists demanded a concrete and observable salvation, beginning here and ending in eternity, including a rather highly codified system of behavior.

The manner in which the Anabaptist emphasis was rejected and the consequent loss of any communication between the Anabaptists and their accusers resulted in the creation of "differential association," by which is meant the "abnormal" communication and interaction with members of the minority as over against others. Thus because of the issues at stake, which led to the feeling that the state churches were either partially or totally blinded to their own biases, and the hostility expressed by the society at large, the interaction with insiders was much higher than would have been expected by chance, had the confrontation not existed. Whether the Anabaptists reluctantly cut off communication, or whether they did so willingly is beside the point; the fact is that they did so.

The strong missionary zeal of the earlier years further tended to mitigate the evolution of the ethnic system, but even so, a missionary rarely incorporates many elements of the pagan society whose members he is trying to convert. In any case, with the increasing decimation and scattering of the Anabaptist flock, there was no other choice but to band together and become the "gathered flock." It will be suggested below that the "gathered" concept emerged alongside or after the actual experience of the emergence of the Anabaptists, but nevertheless evidence seems to suggest that the concept of the gathered church was early considered an important tenet of the faith, even though it was not fully understood.

The gathered church thus became both the expression of the theological beliefs of the Anabaptists, and as the consequence of its minority persecuted position, the source of this view. The continued existence of this group in time created the full-blown ethnic group. The definition of ethnic group for our purposes includes much more than simply the emergence of a common language, common culture, and common theological orientation. "Common to all these objective bases, however, is the social-psychological element of a special sense of both ancestral and future-oriented identification with the group. These are the 'people' of my ancestors, therefore they are my people, and they will be the people of my children and their children."[27] The "people" became more than a group who had a common religious experience; the "people" resembled the Jewish "nation" as described in the Old Testament.

The bare outline of the protest of total ideology by the Anabaptists has been presented. It is not possible to make a conclusive case for it here. But as has been indicated above, the Anabaptist emphases have proved to be hardy, and have evoked numerous testimonies indicating that they were on the right track.[28] What could explain the emergence of a "divergent view," one which challenged the submission to total ideology? Were the Anabaptists imbued with an exceptional gift of perception? Were they superhuman prophets? Was the movement a historical accident, never to be repeated again?

A careful look at some of the objective characteristics of the Anabaptist movement will give us a clue regarding their ability to develop a diverging view, which was at least less the function of their conditions than that of Zwingli. The traditional interpretation has been that the Anabaptists, being poor peasants, simply revolted against their servile position, and anticipated the Marxian revolt of the proletariat — once their eyes were opened to their objective position. From this perspective has come the "disinherited sect" view which suggests that sects emerge from the economically deprived and that they will disappear as soon as the economic conditions improve.[29] The "sectarian disinherited" theory of Anabaptism has been thoroughly discounted by recent research. The earliest Anabaptists represented a broad cross section of their social order.

Therefore this does not answer the question as to how and why the "eyes were opened" in the first place as to their objective conditions. Several significant sociological factors seem to be important in the early Anabaptist movement. The first is that the leaders of the Anabaptist movement were men who were not in high position of authority in the church or in government. They were humanistic scholars, young preachers in the Roman church, or persons with rather average occupations. Therefore they had little to lose in proposing change. The second is that there was no strong charismatic leadership, even though several men appear to have been the spokesmen on numerous occasions. Whenever the original conflict between the reformers and the Anabaptists is described, the Anabaptists are referred to in terms of a group opposing the reformers. It is significant that the reformers do not generally refer to single individuals when they refer to the Anabaptists; rather, they are referred to in a group such as the *Wiedertäufer, Schwärmer,* or *Rottengeister.*[30]

These factors have been influential in producing a basic theological tenet among Anabaptists and a style of operation which forms the heart of the argument proposed here. The non-establishment origin of the leaders of the Anabaptist movement and the group nature of the movement led them to stress the concept of brotherhood, which Troeltsch and others have said was so significantly typical of the Anabaptists. The Anabaptist movement has stressed a concept of the church as a gathered people, a covenanted community, in which everything is centered in the gathering of a people around the presence of Christ.

Franklin Littell quotes with approval Friedmann's characterization of the Anabaptists:

> Now then, the central idea of Anabaptism, the real dynamite in the age of Reformation, as I see it, was this, that one cannot find salvation without caring for his brother, that this "brother" actually matters in the personal life. This interdependence of men gives life and salvation a new meaning. It is not "faith alone" which matters (for which faith no church would be needed) but it is brotherhood, this intimate caring for each other, as it was commanded to the disciples of Christ as the way to God's kingdom. That was the discovery which made Anabaptism so forceful and outstanding in all of church history.[31]

At another place Littell asserts:

The Anabaptist rediscovery of peoplehood and rejection of the institutionalized mass establishment, their reassertion of the biblical role of the laity and the local congregation, were related to a view of history which I have elsewhere termed "primitivism."[32]

Thus, the Anabaptists formed a "community of discipleship" which is "the needed word and witness today."[33] Although this idea cannot be fully discussed here, it illustrates most powerfully a basic sociological understanding that our thought patterns are to a large part determined by our objective surroundings. Emile Durkheim first introduced the idea that the theology of a group is derived from the group's own structure. The "egalitarian" nature of the early Anabaptist movement hence should have produced a theology which stressed such concepts as brotherhood and the significance of the laity.[34]

Although the emphasis on community relates to our basic theme, the important fact is that the Anabaptists developed a new form of theologizing and thought: the group or community nature of thought.

The Anabaptist "divergent conception" can therefore be seen as having been group-initiated and group-derived. Rather than being the result of an individual "charismatic" person such as Luther or Zwingli, Anabaptism proceeded to develop on the basis of a "group charisma." This is in further contrast to most of the Reformation movements, or of other religious movements in the West for that matter. Being aware of the susceptibility to particular ideology of individuals in a social context, the Anabaptists maintained that the Spirit reveals Himself to persons in a group, in which each submits his insights to the group's discernment. Thus, the individual charismatic was absent among them; in fact, it was rejected.

Conrad Grebel, the alleged leader of the first Anabaptists, was clearly not a leader who was trying to obtain a following. Fritz Blanke, one of the most knowledgeable scholars, suggests that one of Grebel's first acts after the Anabaptist movement had taken form, was to write a "letter to Thomas Müntzer in Thuringia, in the name of his circle of friends in Zurich" (p. 59). In almost all the references to the Anabaptists, Blanke refers to them as "Grebel and his friends" (p. 60) or "Blaurock and his friends."[35] In fact, the baptism that sealed the first Anabaptists was a plural affair where Grebel baptized Blaurock and the latter baptized the rest. Menno says, "I have been called unworthily to this office by a people who were willing to obey Christ and His word, who in the fear of God led devoted lives, served their neighbors in love, bore the cross of persecution, sought the welfare and salvation of all men."[36] Note that the group identified and installed the leader, rather than the more normal process of a leader forming a group around his "charisma."

The Reformation leaders do not speak of the followers of Menno Simons, or of Conrad Grebel, although, significantly enough, we can read contemporary accounts of the followers of Jan van Leiden and Dirk Phillips, both of whom were charismatic leaders of groups of schismatic Anabaptists. The theologizing which produced the Anabaptists took place in the context of a group-discerning process — a binding and loosing which involved every person who had committed himself to the group's way. The individual contribution was submitted to the group, tested, and, if usable, integrated into the common core of faith. This may account for the fact that so many confessions of faith were produced by early Anabaptism.

One other argument on the "group nature" of early Anabaptist theologizing can briefly be mentioned, namely, the stress on congregational autonomy and the concept of the church of Christ as a brotherhood — a *laos*. The refusal to accept the priestly status and its functions, the intent to involve all the members of the church in decisions and implementation of the faith, seems to argue strongly that the truth of faith was in the submission of the individual to the body of Christ.

The Anabaptist movement became flexible and expanded rapidly over the face of Western Europe precisely because it was not a movement headed by one charismatic leader who needed to oversee and organize the movement. Rather, it was a movement which spread, and needed only the small and almost furtive fellowship meeting in caves and barns to give direction and motivation to the cause. As has been indicated, Anabaptism was a strong missionary movement and the main reason it came to nought was the thorough decimation it suffered through persecutions.

The schismatic tendencies of individual charisma and the subsequent problems of the transfer of charisma to a new leader, as well as the problem of the routinization of charisma, were not operative in the Anabaptist movement, since it was the creation of group dynamics and responsive to any shifts in the structure of the groups or in the environment. The social source of thought and perception, to say nothing of symbolization, was derived from the interaction of persons who were sharing a common fate, who had committed themselves to a common goal, and who experienced a common relationship to the surrounding world.[37]

That the Anabaptists realized the danger of total ideology in others seems fairly clear from the evidence. But what objective proof do they provide that they themselves were not the victims of total ideology? Although they were quick to point out total ideology in others, did it ever dawn on them that they themselves might also have been totally seduced and blind? The solution to this problem was exceptionally simple:

> We believe, recognize, and confess that the Holy Scriptures both of the Old and New Testaments are to be described as commanded by God and written through holy persons who were driven thereto by the Spirit of God. For this reason the believing born-again Christians are to employ them for teaching and admonishing, for reproof and reformation, to exhibit the foundations of their faith that it is in conformity with Holy Scripture.[38]

The quotation above is from a confession of the Swiss Brethren written in Hesse in 1568. Menno Simons, leader of the Dutch wing of Anabaptism, said, "the whole Scriptures, both of the Old and New Testament, were written for our instruction, admonition, and correction. . . . They are the true scepter and rule by which the Lord's kingdom . . . and congregation must be ruled and governed."[39] It seems clear, therefore, that the safeguard the Anabaptists used was dependence üpon an objective and transcendent source, the Holy Scriptures. Whereas the reformers placed themselves individually above the Scriptures and interpreted thcm, according to the Anabaptists the true way was to view the Scriptures as divine and transcendent and to insist that only under the Spirit's guidance in the disciplined community could an entire group be protected from total ideology.

Secondly, the Anabaptist understanding of epistemology (how one knows and knows what one knows), dependent upon a transcendent source of knowledge, was premised on the interpretation of that source not through individualistic and subjective experience, but through the crucible of the nurture and admonition of the group. Thus, group membership had consisted of persons who were committed to the same goals and who were aware of the dangers of individual ideology and hence protected themselves from individual ideology by submitting themselves to the judgment of others. Since they were aware of the individual sources of distortion and deception, their interpretation of something as holy as the transcendent source of knowledge could not be left to individual whims, but had to be entrusted to the reasoned and balanced insight of the group in a collective search.

Figure 2

Paradigm of Anabaptist and Reformer Cognitive Processes

Anabaptists	Reformers
Bible — Transcendent and final	Bible — Must be interpreted
⬇	⬇
Group — Discerns its meaning	Individual — Interprets
⬇	⬇ (Priest-theologian)
Group — Applies what is discerned	Individual — Applies

On the other hand, the reformers, while accepting the importance of the Scriptures, were consciously and/or unconsciously interpreting the Scriptures to fit the conditions which they

103

were trying to achieve.

So convinced were the early Anabaptists that they were right and all others wrong, that they marched willingly and courageously to the stake to be burned and torn apart. Short of pure fanaticism and group hypnotism, the only explanation for their acceptance of persecution must be an overwhelming and overarching conviction that they were right and all others were wrong. A profusion of documentation illustrates this conviction. A Testament from Bartholomeus Panten delivered to his little daughter after he was put to death in 1592 reads: "Thus, my dear child, lay this to heart, and when you attain to your understanding, it is my fatherly request of you, that you will join yourself to those that fear God, who are by far the least among all people, but yet are the true congregation and church of God, who regulate themselves according to the ordinances of the Lord."[40]

The argument in this chapter is at the heart of the idea of the free church. Whether this interpretation of the Anabaptists is correct remains to be tested by further scholarship, research, and living. What can be asserted with considerable justification is the fact that particular and total ideology can be averted within certain limits, and that the Anabaptists possessed the structures that protected them so that they were able to be more free than many if not most of their contemporaries.

The Precariousness of the Free Church Vision

The vision of a church that was at least relatively free from self-delusion was briefly described in the last chapter. But it was also suggested that the Anabaptists have not been able to maintain their earlier intention. It is instructive to study how a group which was able at one point to protest total ideology later tended to become victim to it. Rather than remaining at an abstract level, it is useful to look at the development of some aspects of Anabaptism to see how the vision of the free church fared.

Although the evidence[1] still needs to be gathered and evaluated, it is clear that the Mennonites have lost their "free church" stance (the term used here to denote the rejection of conditional knowledge)! The best-documented branch is the Dutch church, which serves as a prototype for the rest; it is described as follows:

> The first group (the Dutch branch) is aptly described by Troeltsch's comments on the nonresistant persecuted sects. Based on the Protestant ethic of the "calling" they have all developed into groups which, in the sociological sense, must be described as "bourgeois," and which therefore accept existing conditions. . . . The decline of nonresistance among Dutch Mennonites lay in sociological pressures on the Mennonite community, which altered their status in relation to the "world." . . . They acquired many ideas from other sects tolerated in Holland during the seventeenth century, such as the Socinians, Collegiants, and Remonstrants. The traditional nonresistance became a liberal type of pacifism, which disappeared with the crisis of conscription. Second, becoming wealthy, their concern for purity and simplicity declined, and many of the wealthy, married into non-Mennonite families. Third, the growth of religious toleration in Holland seems to have mitigated the uniqueness of the Mennonites, and they came to assume the expected religious characteristics of the bourgeoisie to which they belonged.[2]

In a significant article entitled "Anabaptist Conception of the Church in the Russian Mennonite Environment," Robert Kreider makes the rather astounding assertion that the Russian Mennonite conception of the state had some striking resemblances to the *Volkskirche:*

A major thesis of this study is that the Mennonite Church in the Russian Mennonite environment moved in the direction and exhibited many of the characteristics of the *Volkskirche* or what the English call the "parish pattern of life." . . . Appraised from the perspective of the Anabaptist conception of the church, the Mennonites in Russia forfeited at the outset the possibility of being a brotherhood-type church. They had to suppress the missionary imperative of the gospel. . . . Furthermore, they accepted a system of privileges which were bound to qualifications, not of faith, but of blood. . . . [3]

Kreider suggests that some experts on Russian Mennonite history have advocated the recognition of the inevitability and necessity of an "*ecclesiola* in *ecclesia*," a *Kerngemeinde* within the *Volkskirche*. [4]

The Old Colony Mennonites, an offshoot of the Russian Mennonites, offer considerable support for the contention that Kreider makes, namely, that the Anabaptists-Mennonites have slowly gone through the process of becoming a *Volkskirche*, which means they are becoming like the church they were protesting in the Reformation. But before the actual material can be presented, it will be necessary to identify briefly the essentials of original Anabaptism in order to see how it has changed.

The Anabaptist "charter" has not yet been definitively established, although an increasing amount of literature is contributing to a consensus. It becomes necessary, therefore, to become a "partisan" and to select what appears to the author to be the best coherent treatment of the charter so far. Most recognized authorities on Anabaptism agree that the Anabaptists believed that the kingdom of God was to be attempted here and now. At the conclusion of his justly famous *The Anabaptist Vision*, Harold S. Bender says, "The Anabaptist vision was not a detailed blueprint for the reconstruction of the human society, but the Brethren did believe that Jesus intended that the kingdom of God should be set up in the midst of earth, here and now, and this they proposed to do forthwith." [5]

In similar language, Robert Friedmann says, "To the

Anabaptists 'salvation' (or rather redemption) means the newly acquired strength to walk the narrow path and to know oneself as a part of the divine drama which will eventually lead to the kingdom of God on earth."[6] Another more objective authority on Anabaptism, Roland Bainton, implies that Anabaptists attempted to establish the kingdom of God:

> The Anabaptist view rested upon pessimism with regard to the world and optimism with regard to the church. The world — that is, society at large — will always be the part of the flesh and the devil, but the church must walk another road and must exemplify within her fellowship the living and dying of the Lord Jesus. She must be a community of saints whose members, though not perfect, yet aspire to perfection and strive mightily.[7]

What were the central traits of the kingdom of God? Bainton says the "kernel of Anabaptism was an ethical urge."[8] Friedmann, whose quotations above already intimate as much, suggests in innumerable places that the Anabaptists stressed a "stark biblical dualism."[9] This dualism implied a rejection of "the fallen world of darkness and sin." He had to separate from it and begin a new life — not alone, to be sure, but together with fellow believers, his brethren, forming a church (*Gemeinde*) of renewed Christians, a fellowship of committed disciples.[10]

This theme is strongly emphasized in Bender's statement, for in it he suggests that the Anabaptists' emphasis was an ethical one: "To them it was unthinkable for one truly to be a Christian without creating a new life on divine principles both for himself and for all men who commit themselves to the Christian way."[11] He continues: "For the Anabaptists, the church was neither an institution (Catholicism), nor the instrument of God for the proclamation of the divine Word (Lutheranism), nor a resource group for individual piety (Pietism). It was a brotherhood of love in which the fullness of the Christian life ideal is to be expressed."[12]

The Anabaptist concept of the life in the kingdom of God meant the following response in behavior: (1) radical ethical obedience to the commands of Christ; (2) separation from the renegade world; (3) nurture of the Christian "covenant community"; (4) a mission, not that of bringing the gospel to the world, but of calling men to join the community.

The first point has been sufficiently documented in the introduction above. Separation from the world has profuse historical support in the objective life of the "peculiar people" observable wherever Anabaptists have lived. The nurture of the Christian community has included a vast array of activities ranging from edification and excommunication to the development of mutual aid and burial aid societies, which have been perpetuated in various forms to the present time. The final behavior response, a missionary thrust that was "conventional" directed, has not received adequate analysis.

That the Anabaptists were the first and greatest missionaries of the Reformation period has been well established.[13] What has not been adequately stressed is that their missionary thrust was to incorporate nonbelievers into the covenant community, so that as soon as a person believed, he was baptized into a fellowship and subordinated to its discipline and care. This is clearly implied in John Horsch's account of a young church:

> In 1557 a member of the established Protestant church of Strasburg in Alsace visited a meeting of the Swiss Brethren near that city. A number of persons were being received into the church by baptism on that occasion. Among the questions addressed to the applicants before the ordinance was administered was this, Whether they, if necessity required it, would devote all their possessions to the service of the brotherhood, and would not fail any member that is in need, if they were able to render aid.[14]

Although he does not elaborate, Bainton implies the same when he says: "Their theory (the Anabaptists) of the church made of it a conventicle and not a church of the community. Christianity, they said, demands a quality of living which can be and will be achieved only by heartfelt Christians who have truly died with Christ to sin and risen with Him to newness of life."[15]

The missionary thrusts of Anabaptists therefore must logically be seen as covenanting in the kingdom of God, for it makes little sense to have a concept of the church and of the kingdom of God and then to refute it by promoting a mission which would not build the kingdom of God. The implications of this view will be discussed in the next section. In any case, this essay proposes that the form of the Great Commission among Anabaptists meant calling unregenerate men to repentance into the fellowship of discipleship. It was a call to forsake self-gratifying sin and to turn toward submission to Christ in the covenanted community, and not merely participation in the sacraments.

The Anabaptist behavior which resulted from this "charter" was of such radical nature that it is one of the most misunderstood movements in religious history. In order to be understood, the radicalness of their behavior must therefore be derived from their charter, rather than the other way around. That is, the religious beliefs of the Anabaptists resulted in a consistent system of behavior. Only some of the most important patterns of behavior relevant to the argument presented here can be included.[16]

1. Rejection of the state church. The extensive scholarship that has retrieved the original dynamics of Anabaptism indicates that the original Anabaptists rejected the idea of a church that was supported by the state. Fritz Blanke, a careful student of Anabaptism, says, "They sought a free church in the double sense: a congregation free from the state and based upon voluntary membership."[17] Grebel and his colleagues refused to recognize the *Volkskirche* as the authentic church. This has been a central position and teaching of Anabaptism ever since, and was documented in the preceding chapter.

2. Rejection of participation in state life. Again Blanke states: "But Grebel did not only demand withdrawal from the *Volkskirche;* in the same letter to Müntzer he rejected the participation of the Christian in the life of the state. In the opinion of his group the Christian should accept no civil office or military service."[18] Although there has been some variation, it can be said that Anabaptists have generally avoided participation in the affairs of the state, although they have recognized it and prayed for it.

3. A separated life. The Anabaptists' concept of the kingdom of God and of the church, which they conceived as the means of establishing the kingdom, demanded an absolutist ethic of life, which meant "rejection of all historical relativities. Anabaptism tried to cast aside all historical adaptations to the institutions of society which were regarded as compromise of the pure gospel. Historically this radical criticism placed them against the very structure of the society of the day. . . . "[19] This separated life demanded an absolute and literalistic following of the commands of Christ, which included mutual aid, mutual love, honesty and integrity, sacrificial and simple living, frugality and responsibility.

4. A disciplined community. The Anabaptists stressed absolute obedience, as indicated above. However, because this did not occur in a vacuum, it necessitated a strong binding-loosing process. In fact, it has been proposed that binding and loosing was the central dynamic of Anabaptism, but it is assumed here that it is rather a means to achieve the end of absolute radical obedience described above.[20] The strict discipline which culminated in the excommunication and ban in its extreme form is almost unique with the Mennonite Church, and explains at least in part the schisms that have plagued it.

The first generation Anabaptists have been extensively studied, and from this study the theoretical nature of the movement has been extrapolated. However, this has created considerable difficulty, because only sparse material exists which indicates how the movement was able or unable to incorporate this charter in actual social life later on. Thus the second and succeeding generations' response to the original vision is in need of clarification: How was the original impetus institutionalized? Was the Anabaptist movement able to incorporate and implement in succeeding generations the original thrust?

Because of lack of information this question cannot now be adequately answered in reference to the continuous thread of Anabaptism which derived from the original movement. However, some of the answer can be given by looking carefully at some of the direct descendants of the Anabaptist movement existent today and by making some assumptions, which hopefully will be generally acceptable: (1) A Mennonite group surviving today is in many respects a generic heir to original Anabaptism. (2) A more conservative group has retained more institutionalized aspects of the charter of the original movement than has a liberal one. (3) A rural-traditional group has preserved more of the original institutions than an urbanized and nontraditional group. (4) Since institutions change very slowly, the institutional forms existent at any point in time at least partially represent attempts to preserve an original response to a need.

The Old Colony Mennonites will be used to analyze the question: How well has the Mennonite church-ethnic group been able to achieve its original charter? In view of the assumptions stated above, the Old Colony is a good representative because: (1) it is a surviving descendant of the Anabaptist tradition (via Holland, Prussia, Russia, Canada and Mexico, British Honduras, Bolivia and Paraguay); (2) as one of the most conservative of Mennonite groups, it is motivated to try to conserve the values of original Anabaptism; (3) the Old Colony has consistently been a rural-traditional society and can trace its ancestry through the same type of society to its Anabaptist origins; (4) the Old Colony forms represent attempts to carry on the essence of the Anabaptist tradition — in their own eyes at least, if not in the eyes of others.

A careful analysis of the Old Colony will reveal that it is still concerned with the emphases originally espoused by the Anabaptists. The Old Colony is still actively rejecting the state church. As a matter of fact, its hostility toward the Catholic Church in Mexico, for example, resembles in many ways the attitude displayed by early Anabaptists. To the Old Colony Mennonites Catholics are considered apostate and no more religious than the primitive Indians that still roam the environs of the Old Colony in Mexico. Upon numerous occasions the author asked Old Colonists whether the Catholics could be Christian, and invaribly received the same response: "How can they be Christian? Aren't they the Antichrist?" The Catholic

Church is not the state church in Mexico, but it is the "established" church, which is in all essentials the same thing.

On the second point, nonparticipation in the affairs of the state, the Old Colony probably represents original Anabaptism better than any other Mennonite group today. The state is considered "outside the perfection of Christ" and is simply ignored if possible. When the state must be dealt with, it is confronted in a stance that is reminiscent of early Anabaptism: if the magistracy does not submit to the will of God, emigration is the only recourse. Within the last several years the Mexican government's demands that the Old Colony upgrade its schools have been met with the threat of migration unless the demands were withdrawn. Subsequently they were, at least for the time being.

In reference to the separated life, the Old Colony has illustrated this emphasis as well as any other Mennonite group in history. The Amish are usually cited as the group that has expressed separation from the world in its most uncompromising form. But the Old Colony has done the job more effectively than even the Amish. Whereas the Amish tried to separate themselves from the world culturally and socially, the Old Colony has also separated itself ecologically by living in enclaves where both of the above could be controlled even more drastically. In some cases, in fact, separation has amounted to almost complete isolation from surrounding peoples, as witness the migrations to northern Alberta, British Columbia, British Honduras, Bolivia, and Paraguay. It is irrelevant to argue that their separation from the world was misplaced, that they missed the real meaning of worldliness. The point is that they separated from the world as they interpreted the world. A final definition of "the world" has not yet been conclusively established; in fact, this would appear to be a futile effort.

The fourth emphasis of the disciplined community has been adamantly adhered to in the Old Colony system. The sanctions of the excommunication and ban are still practiced in the Old Colony. But that is only the negative side of a very elaborate and strong group discipline. Beliefs are strictly circumscribed;

there is a great homogeneity in what is believed in the Old Colony. Similarly, all levels of Old Colony behavior presumed to have implications for the religious system are carefully controlled. The schools are carefully directed and watched to assure that only approved information is learned. A monthly meeting of the clergy deals with deviants accused of transgressing Old Colony norms. In short, the disciplined community is so effectively achieved that many Old Colonists believe that very little freedom exists for the individual to express any idiosyncratic traits.

A case can be made for the Old Colony as the best representation of the heir to the genuine Anabaptist heritage. But, paradoxically, rarely if ever has the Old Colony been held up as a model of the Anabaptist tradition. In fact, rarely has the Old Colony been referred to in Anabaptist literature, and where it has been mentioned it is usually, if not always, in a pejorative and disparaging way. What explains this paradox? Are the assumptions stated above thus poorly advised, or is there another explanation?

It has been proposed that the answer to the apparent paradox and to the question of how well the Anabaptist charter has been implemented lies in the following paradoxical proposition: the greater the achievement of the original Anabaptist charter on an empirical level of behavior, the greater the negation of the intent of the charter. Thus, the more the Anabaptists tended to approximate the kingdom of God, the greater their proneness to be the world developed. The Old Colony's life can be analyzed in light of the above paradoxical statement.

The uncompromising rejection of the established or state church by the Old Colony resulted in the development of an established church within the Old Colony system. The traits of the established church and sect are too familiar to warrant extensive treatment. Since Troeltsch elaborated the church-sect typology, the traits of both have been second nature to all scholars. Included in the "sect," or the group that rejected the state church, are: (1) adult voluntary membership; (2) mutual brotherhood; (3) rejection of worldly authority or domination.[21]

In the Old Colony, voluntary adult membership is actually nonexistent. Joining the church is as normal and routine as it ever was in countries where the *Volkskirche* was operative. The total-community life is such that the strictly religious (sacred) aspects cannot be separated from the social and mundane. Thus, an Old Colony youth who grows up on the Old Colony social system naturally becomes a member of the church; it is unheard of to refuse to become a member of the church. In fact, marriage assures membership, for an Old Colony youth cannot get married unless the church performs the ceremony and it will not perform the ceremony until he is a baptized member of the church.

The rejection of involvement in social affairs by the church has boomeranged in the Old Colony. The clergy and its authority coerce the membership all along the line. An individual is not allowed to sell his land to a pagan in Mexico, since the church owns title. The "secular" affairs of the villages are ultimately under the jurisdiction and surveillance of the church. A person who decides to form a partnership with anyone but an Old Colonist is brought into line by the church. A miscreant in village life is punished by the church. The church and the "secular" aspects of life are thoroughly mixed, as much as at the height of the *Corpus Christianum.*

The rejection of involvements with the state has paradoxically created of the Old Colony a little state, with almost every function being carried out in traditional state ways. Since the Old Colony has historically rejected the police function of the state, it has developed its own. Minor infractions of Old Colony norms are handled on an individual basis. More serious disturbances and conflicts are handled by the village governments, composed of the married males in the village who own land — who are themselves an aristocracy reminiscent of Calvin's Geneva.

Numerous times the author has observed conflicts between residents of villages, which often resulted in physical violence and bloodletting. Intervillage disputes create real problems, since there is no secular central government. One of the reasons for this problem is the lack of jurisdictional clarity. Who decides what issue at what level?

Economic processes are handled in much the same way. The allocation of pasture lands, new land, irrigation rights, taxation on land, crops, property, and other functions are taken care of by a simple yet effective bureaucracy. The management of the educational process, although guarded by the clergy, is conducted by the villages in a rather standardized way. Each village hires the teacher, provides for his support, supplies the facilities needed, and makes decision on school days. In short, the Old Colony manages all the activities that a state normally provides for its citizens, except for the creation and maintenance of a military force. However, in some instances Old Colony men have organized to defend raids perpetrated by Mexican nationals.

The Old Colony has pursued the separated life to the absolute limit. But it is clear to most observers of the Old Colony that separation from the world as they define it has been so throughgoing that a new culture, unique and autonomous, has emerged. Separation has resulted in a new form of language, value system, world view, dress patterns, and behavior patterns that is unique, but that is a culture in its own right. In separating themselves from "worldly" beliefs, practices, and things, the Old Colony had to substitute something else, for, being a human society, it found itself unable to avoid cultural patterns. Several illustrations will suffice.

Mixing with "worldly people" in the towns has long been forbidden in the Old Colony, for such things as smoking, drinking, and carousing are clearly signs of apostasy. However, the author has spent many evenings observing Old Colony "faithful" interacting in a not too pious and edifying way in the local stores found in each Old Colony village. Here beer, wine, and other liquor are consumed, drunks are observed, and filthy language and stories are not uncommon. Granted, this behavior is deplored by the clergy, but it occurs nevertheless. Although it would decrease with more external, repressive measures by the "state" as described above, this repression would only increase the "paradox" proposed.

There is supposedly no interaction with "pagan" and degenerate non-Mennonites; open interaction with Mexicans is considered a sign of apostasy. Yet Old Colonists practice an extravagant amount of deceit and hostility. Even though they are members of the same brotherhood, they manifest a considerable degree of distrust and exploitation, with persons often becoming means rather than ends. Therefore a serious challenge can be raised as to how successful the Old Colony has been in separating itself from the "world" — as the Old Colony itself defines it — for it has become the world!

The Old Colony has probably achieved a greater degree of discipline among its members than in most other Anabaptist groups. Almost without exception Old Colonists have refused to participate in state activities, have separated themselves from the life of the world, and have participated in the "voluntary" religion. Uniformity in belief and in behavior is amazing. The normative system has become so completely internalized that a person who deviates feels very guilty and is sternly disciplined by the informal operation of sanctions of disapproval.

Yet, paradoxically, this discipline has created a pattern in which although there is outward conformity, there is often private nonconformity. Many cases of this nonconformity can be cited. One such is the prohibition of electricity. But many farmers have installed it in their barns and in their kitchens. Thus, when a minister or bishop comes to visit, he is carefully taken to the front room and not allowed to come into the kitchen where he would see the deviance. A discernible cynicism operates, in which conformity is calculated and highly tentative, without any commitment to the reasons for the stipulated pattern.

The Old Colony saga reminds the observer of the children of Israel. They were the chosen people, yet their end was always that of falling out of favor with God. Instead of remaining a "people of God," they continually fell into the trap of wanting to become a nation "like other nations." The Jews misunderstood God and took the road of becoming a political

117

power rather than a people whose king was God Himself. In like manner, the Old Colony strove mightily to live up to its covenant with God, but in the process became an earthly kingdom, even though they rejected the political dimension which the Jews accepted. So in a sense, even though the Old Colony resisted disobedience by not taking the route the Jews took (the political state) the Old Colony became a "state" precisely in the process of attempting to avoid it. Even though the Old Colony resisted taking earthly power into their own hands, it nevertheless turned out that way.

The paradox stands out in bold relief: The attempt to consistently put principles into practice serves to predestine the Old Colony to corruption and captivity. Or to the degree that the religious movement achieves its charter, to the same degree it refutes these principles. In the language of Karl Mayer, the imparting of the spirit in concrete forms destroys the essence that is sought. Thus, the Old Colony cannot be advanced as the best exhibit of the achievement and preservation of the free church vision. What can explain this paradox?

Numerous theories attempt to explain the way utopian protest groups have succumbed to baser motivations and have lost their original lofty ideals. Many of these theories are intuitive, highly plausible, and certainly partial answers to the question. But they are only partial answers.

One of the most pervasive theories to explain the failure of achievement is the Christ-culture concept, popularized by H. Richard Niebuhr.[22] In this framework the problem of the loss of the prophetic aspect of the Christian church can be explained by a variation in the way the Christian understands the relation of Christ to the temporal order (culture). Niebuhr suggests that the Mennonites have been one of the best illustrations of the Christ against culture stance, in which culture is of no relevance to the church. In this orientation the intention is to live as faithfully as possible within the community, ignoring the fact that Christ is indeed concerned about culture.

Another interpretation suggests that the sect-type groups have typically taken the "withdrawal from culture" position. In this view, the "church is composed of a group of believers who are summoned to come apart from the profane world of business, politics, liberal education, public entertainment, and war in order to establish a separate community of the elect."[23] Under the "folk church" Niebuhr includes those groups that "support and sanctify the highest ideals and noblest institutions of a particular culture or subcultural group. In Germany prior to World War II the Lutheran Church became such a *Volkskirche*."[24]

Gardner champions a third alternative, which he calls the "Pattern of Creative Tension." He suggests that the "concept of the church and secular culture as existing in permanent tension attempts to take into account both the yes and the no that always need to be spoken by the church to culture. The sect, 'the church against the world,' addresses only an unequivocal 'No!' to the world. The parallelist church fails to enter into any real communication with culture. The folk church, on the other hand, speaks only an unqualified 'Yes!' to secular society. In contrast to all of these, the church that interacts with culture seeks to maintain a relationship of polar and dynamic tension between the church and society."[25]

Many other treatments of the church-world have been presented and propounded. All of them tend to follow the same pattern: creation of typologies that attempt to classify groups according to their stance toward culture, and then a proposal for a typology that would be the "correct" stance between the transcendental and the secular or mundane. They are all inadequate because of the "ideological" captivity under which they have been proposed. In the first place, the Christ-culture relationship is normally propounded by an individual scholar who feels some concern about the "relevance" of the Christian faith. Most scholars who have written about relevance have not recognized that the very concept of relevance is an ideological one, a subtle, but pervasive norm in our culture. To argue about the essence of Christianity using the ethnocentric concepts of a particular culture (relevance) is not the most fruitful way to interpret Christ's message!

The related point that the whole problem has normally been propounded by individual scholars in the typically individualistic, rational method runs counter to what has been proposed above as the way in which individuals can free themselves from total ideology. This should be sufficiently obvious by now to need no further elaboration.

A third and possibly most significant point is that the Christ-culture dimension is precisely not the issue for those Anabaptist groups and other groups which have at some point achieved a relatively free church status. The Anabaptists never condemned culture, not even the Old Colonists, who certainly would be classified as "Christ against culture" by such scholars as Niebuhr. The true free church has always been concerned about "hearing the Word of God and obeying it." For the free church groups, culture has always been the means to obedience, even though, as illustrated in the Old Colony, numerous confusions have developed. For the free church, the typology would be, "Christ the Lord of Culture." It is significant that the typologies have never included this concept, precisely because for many long generations in Christendom at large the lordship of Christ over everything is the very thing that has been rejected.

As this volume has intimated from time to time, the free church idea has come to life in various places and at various times. One proponent of the free church has written a moving book in which he speaks squarely to the Christ-culture issue:

> I had learned in Crainie beyond all doubting that the church is always being re-born in these companies of the few, but was only beginning to understand the travail of its re-birth. For we who are called to take no reckoning of success are ourselves placed where success is expected of us; we who are to count the world well lost for Christ's sake are ourselves looked to for the maintaining of the church's position in the world. [26]

The basic problem lies in the temptation of the "fallacy of misplaced concretion" — the loss of the single eye, in Jesus' terms. As a representative of a thoroughgoing tradition, the

Old Colony has become a victim of its own environmental conditions and has been seduced by them. The full explanation for the precariousness of the free church vision cannot be given here. Why a group becomes a victim of its environment is the critical question. In the following chapter an attempt to answer this question will be discussed.

It is sobering that a group that has protested the seduction by the values of secular society can itself become seduced by these very values as it tries to live by the values of the kingdom of God. The implications of this fact for the theology of the Christian church, especially as it relates to perfectability, eschatology, and salvation, are vast.

The Requirements for a Free Church

With the discussion of the nature of particular and total ideology, and with a case study of the development of ideology completed, the question that immediately remains is, "Lord, who then shall be saved?" If the Anabaptist tradition, presented as an example of the rejection of secular seduction, has in many cases succumbed itself, what, if indeed anything, can be done to avoid such seduction? What are the basic requirements necessary for a contemporary group of Christians to extricate themselves from a total ideology and to preserve the freedom once it is achieved?

One basic orientation supporting the arguments in this volume is that the free church concept can best be defined as that group of Christians (congregation, denomination, or segment of the Christian tradition) which has not been blinded by the values and goals of its environment, so that it is literally free to represent the kingdom of God to a rebellious and alien world. Notice the "represent" not "be." The intent of the discussion is not to suggest that the "free church" has been perfect or free from sin.

On the contrary, it has been aware of its own sinfulness, and has been aware of how its own life and very thought patterns have been conditioned, but recognizes that this is contrary to the will of God. It has been free from a basic self-delusion about its own status regarding sinlessness. Thus, when a group of Anabaptists and related groups got together and produced a statement that "War is contrary to the will of God," it was not a statement of perfection but a confession that they had been freed to see what their position on war could and should be!

Earlier and more complete definitions of the free church have dealt with its basic refusal to be allied and subservient to the state, to be free from state control or direction.[1] Beyond this important requirement, the free church concept has referred to the nature of the church itself; that is, to the voluntary or non-coerced nature of membership in the body of Christ.[2] The free church tradition has stressed the voluntary nature or constitution of the body of Christ, whereas the post-Constantine

Volkskirche model assumed that all persons in a political-geographic area (parish, in later times) were automatically members of the local visible church.[3] On the contrary, the free church has stressed the importance of the biblical reality that a man must be free to be a pagan, and that only upon mature and willing response to the moving of the Spirit does a man attach himself to a fellowship of believers.[4]

A fuller view of the free church, one closer to the position taken in this volume, includes the freedom from "culture religion." Culture religion is that system of quasi-religion which has identified with the basic values of the society and has succeeded in harmonizing the religious message and the situational characteristics. Thus, American sociologists have little difficulty in showing how, for example, stratification, ethnic factors, racial and political factors have divided the church into a patchwork quilt with practically no interaction between the various segments.[5] One illustration of American "culture religion" will suffice. The following table combines a number of factors sociologists normally use to show the way the Christian church is "split" along lines mentioned above.

Table 2
Sociological Characteristics and Denominations*

Religious Group and Race	% $2,000 and Above	% S if Employed	% in High Status Occupation	Median School Year Completed	% in Three or more Formal Groups
White					
Catholic	27	7	19	10.0	14
Episcopalian	35	9	42	12.5	42
Lutheran	30	6	28	12.2	17
Calvinist	35	11	37	12.5	21
Methodist	32	8	27	12.3	23
Baptist	21	6	15	9.8	8
Small Sects	16	11	17	9.5	9
No Denomination	29	11	26	12.0	17
Semi-Christian	24	15	39	12.4	19
Jewish	42	41	62	12.5	45
Eastern Orthodox	35	15	13	9.3	8
No Preference	23	9	28	10.0	7
Negro					
Catholic	6	4	7	10.0	8
Methodist	7	5	6	9.8	12
Baptist	8	3	6	9.1	7
Other	12	10	15	9.8	10

*Source: Albert J. Meyer and Harry Sharp, "Religious Preference and Worldly Success," *American Sociological Review*, Volume 27 (April 1962), p. 225.

Although this table includes an enormous amount of information, only a few bits can be lifted out. Episcopalians, Calvinists, and Unitarians are ranked high in economic status, although Jews rank even higher. The sect groups and the Negro groups rank universally lower. Education tends to follow the same track. The status of occupation is also clearly identified by denominational membership. The last column, which reveals the extent to which members of a particular denomination belong to formal associations, shows some significant differences. As will be shown later, the degree to which the individual is tied in with groups tends to indicate the degree to which the individual is integrated and related to others in ways that bring meaning and stability.

In any case, the significant thing to notice is that the religious denominations reflect education, economic and social divisions and structures just as the bulk of society does. Christian churches hence are stratified churches, having little in common and having different "views" of reality because of their differing positions in the social fabric.

But the sociological variables attest only to a deeper identification of God and country. There is little need to document how the "national church" has almost universally identified its own purpose and existence with the goals and identity of the nation. A recent analysis of the Billy James Hargis documents illustrates the confusion of Christian and nationalist ideas, purposes, and convictions.[6] Martin Luther's support of the "Christian princes" in their attempt to suppress the Reformation sects and the National Association of Evangelicals' approval of the American military intervention in Vietnam are in essence the same thing. They express the Christian's delusion that Christ's "kingdom is of this world."

The deepest meaning of the free church refers, however, to that group of Christians which not only refuses to be taken in by the "mould of the world," but which is aware of its own fallibility and hence structures itself so that it can be protected from its own self-deception. The free church, therefore, is the church which not only has become aware of its own sinfulness and dependency upon God, but which has responded by obediently taking up the cross of self-denying obedience. Put in sociological terminology, it has yielded its own structure of reality for one that is divinely ordered. The divine order is the only order that can allow man to follow Christ in obedience. But the divine order is achieved only as Christians covenant together to let God's order operate. Only that Christian group which allows itself to be divinely structured will be free to see the world as God sees it, and be free to obey.[7]

Ironically, the "sons of darkness" are wiser than the "sons of light." Of the many possible examples of "secular" attempts to achieve true "freedom" as here defined, only several can be given. For instance, the medical profession has long maintained the practice of having a female nurse present when a male doctor examines a female patient. The medical profession, realizing that its male practitioners are humans with normal weaknesses, has taken a step toward the divine order by structuring its procedures so that temptations and seduction of a more physical variety may at least be attenuated. In the business world, the countersignature of checks is only one of many techniques used to bolster the moral integrity and honor of its citizens. It should be noted, however, that all of these attempts are always only weak and partial realizations of the desired behavior.

Only in the Christian faith do we forget man's need for "freedom" and allow him to become involved in his own subjectivism and self-deceptive rationalization. In the era when the fear of hell was a strong deterrent there may have been some external assistance to become free, although it is highly doubtful. But certainly since the advent of western individualism each individual by the very structure of culture has become the victim of his own subjective perception and his selfish gratifications. Hence personal as well as public morality is a matter of private relationship to God. A Christian's financial matters are not the business of anyone else; one's sexual and erotic activities are things only God knows about.

Small wonder then that with individuals trapped in their own subjectivity, which is in turn interlaced with the subjection of others, the Christian church can condone and support war; can condone and support amassing of wealth for personal gratification; can enslave others (even fellow Christians) to produce for their own selfish needs; and can be unconcerned about the plundering of natural resources and beauty. When the Christian's life is structured so that he is not freed from his own egotism, the entire theological apparatus as well as the perception of reality is warped and tainted. The Christian who believes that war can be conducted under the blessing of God is a prisoner, shackled in his own spiritually dark cave.[8] A church that cannot help him see his error is in the same dark prison. A congregation or a denomination that does not provide for the destruction of subjective self-deceit on the individual or group level is apostate; in fact, is the Antichrist!

The Apostle Paul epitomizes the issue when he says, "Wretched man that I am! who shall deliver me out of the body of this death" (Romans 7:24)? It is the author's contention that he was already a free church Christian, for in the verses immediately preceding he says, "But if what I would not, that I do, I consent unto the law that it is good. So now it is no more I that do it, but sin which dwelleth in me. For I know that in me, that is, in my flesh, dwelleth no good thing: for to will is present with me, but to do that which is good is not" (Romans 7:16-18). Paul's admission of self-deceit and his obvious insistent dependence upon the church enabled him to become a leader in the prophetic stream that has blessed him to this day.

The discussion so far has not made reference to the possibility that a transcendent power, the Holy Spirit, is the key issue in the entire matter of total ideology. Without spending too much time in developing this theme, it can be observed that dependence upon the working of the Holy Spirit is imperative, and the absolute starting point. Without the power of the Holy Spirit, everything is of no avail. But the Holy Spirit can only work if He is allowed access. The Holy Spirit should not be blamed for the seduction of the church throughout its history! The question is one of submission to its bidding.

What must the church do in order to yield to the will of God to become a free church? First, it must depend on and submit to the Spirit of God. Then it must recognize its own self-deception and structure its social relations so that it will be protected from further self-deception. This can't be done by a massive reorganization of the Christian church, for that is patently impossible anyhow. For instance, notice the extreme difficulty with which the church ever changes, in spite of enormous energy spent in study conferences and the like.

The free church will emerge only as small groups of Christians here and there launch out in the manner of Abraham, leaving kindred and friends and going to a land promised by God. The only way the Christian church will leave its unfreedom is to organize small Christian groups in a manner that will allow them to become free churches. The following discussion therefore refers to the strategy of small groups of Christians, such as koinonia groups or small congregations. It is based on the sociological premise that group structures influence the cognitive and behavior processes of individuals.

Social relations have always had length, depth, and width. That is to say, first of all, that human relations among people vary in their length of duration. Thus, an interaction between a sales clerk and a purchaser may last for three minutes and after this these two may never meet again. On the other extream is the duration of the interaction between husband

Figure 3
The Length Dimension in Social Interaction
Secondary Type Relationship   Primary Type Relationship

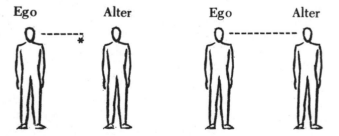

Ego   Alter   Ego   Alter

*The broken line indicates interaction in all the figures.
**The length of the line indicates the length of the interactions.

128

and wife who have been married for fifty years.

Human relations also vary in the degree of depth-intimacy. The length of two sets of interrelationships may be generally similar, such as a relationship with a neighbor and one with a brother. But the degree of intimacy and sharing is greatly different. The neighbor may not even know where you went on your last vacation, but the brother knows about you innermost hostilities and apprehensions.

Figure 4
The Depth Dimension in Social Interaction
Secondary Type Relationship   Primary Type Relationship

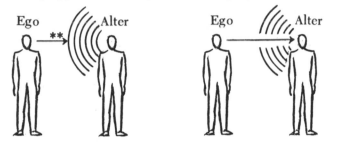

Ego   Alter   Ego   Alter

°°The concentric circles indicate defenses and masks put up by individuals.

The breadth of interrelationships with others also varies tremendously. One sees a colleague at work only as a fellow employee, although greater intimacy can and often does develop which touches at other roles, such as his problems with drink. But the relationship of a man and wife cuts across all roles and positions. Hence a wife relates to her husband as housekeeper, lover, mother of their children, and partner in community activities. A pastor's relationship with a parishioner also is of greater breadth than that of colleagues at work, although it is less broad than that of husband and wife. (See Figure 5.)

The length, depth, and breadth of human relationships are therefore the framework within which human society enfolds itself. Human relations have a length dimension (duration), a depth dimension (the psychic-emotional), and a breadth dimension (the social role). The individual's relationship

129

Figure 5
The Breadth Dimension in Social Interaction
Secondary Type Relationship   Primary Type Relationship

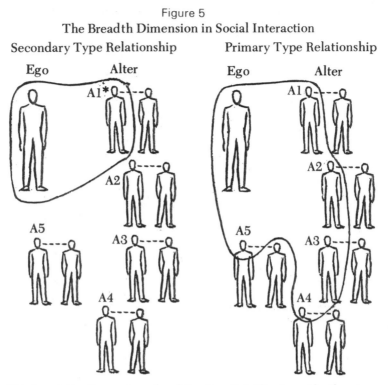

*A1-5 symbolize the varying role relationships that Alter has with other structures.

with others in his social environment can thus differ along three dimensions. If he relates in a minimal degree to others on all three dimensions, he is an isolated, subjective asocial being. He is relating in a world that has been termed *Gesellschaft*-like, or secondary. The person whose relationships on the three dimensions are extended to their fullest possible is a participant in a primary *Gemeinschaft* type of social relationship.

The more unattached an individual is to others on all three dimensions, the more he exhibits the alienation that is being documented on every hand. On the contrary, the more he is related on three dimensions to others, the more he is integrated into society. Obviously, the number of people that one can

130

relate to declines as a person tends toward the primary type of relationship within the three dimensions.

Modern industrial society has tended to move from primary to secondary relationships. Considerable confusion as to the meaning of the change still exists. In many ways the freedom and mobility of secondary relationships are truly liberating and emancipating of the human spirit. But from other perspectives, the relationship produces the opposite — alienated and unstable persons and unstable institutional structures.

The Christian, however, has little choice but to opt for the primary type of relationship, for the Christian gospel talks about loving and caring, about going the second mile, and about forgiving seventy times seven. This type of activity is not possible where the relationship exists for one fleeting moment in a lifetime, or is narrowed down to a one-role relationship, or never penetrates beneath the impersonal masks everyone wears in public. It is only in the primary relationship that the Christian gospel can become effective. Christ may have had seventy disciples at one time, but it appears that He eventually narrowed them down to twelve for this simple reason.

For anything to happen, therefore, in the Christian church the dimensions mentioned above must be kept in mind. The relationships must have length, depth, and breadth. But before we discuss what the forms are that allow for length, breadth, and depth in human relationships in the context of the church, let us first find out what is the objective of the Christian church.

Although the definitive description of the Christian church (the body of Christ) is not central to our argument, a few things must be said about it in order for us to understand how the free church relates to it and how it protects the central functions of the Christian church. The description of the church will be presented in brief outline form, and will approach the problem from a functional perspective — what the church *does*, not what it is.[9]

The Functions of the Body of Christ:
A. The body of Christ is a worshiping and fellowshiping body.
   1. It engages in acts of praising God for His wonderful acts.

2. It engages in prayer of thanksgiving and adoration as well as petition.
3. It engages in forms of reaffirmation through song, testimony, and other symbolic acts, the dedication and commitment made to God.

B. The body of Christ is a witnessing body.
   1. It confesses the lordship of Christ, the judgment of God, and all the other aspects of God's acts in history.
   2. It preaches the lordship of Christ outside the congregation to those who do not understand and/or know about it.
   3. It prophesies by pronouncing the "word from the Lord" for the hour, warning the world of God's work and will.

C. The body of Christ is a reconciling body.
   1. It engages in mutual forgiveness of one another, confronting each other with faults and participating in the forgiveness Christ has offered them.
   2. It is a restoring fellowship, where the sin is not only confessed and forgiven, but where the person is healed of his sin so that he will not sin again.
   3. It is a forbearing fellowship in which the sins and weaknesses of the other person become each one's concern, just as Christ became the "man for others."

D. The body of Christ is a serving body.
   1. It first shares with members of the household of faith, but beyond that it shares unreservedly with all needy everywhere.
   2. It further involves itself in an organized and ordered way in meeting human need, as was done in the Jerusalem congregation.
   3. It not only serves immediate needs, it also becomes involved in the long-term rehabilitation of men and their institutions so that the evils need not continue and demand incessant service.

E. The body of Christ is a teaching body.
   1. It is concerned about transmitting the good news to the offspring of its own members.

2. It is concerned about informing its own offspring and others what the nature and content of the gospel is.

3. It is involved in exposition and elucidation of the meaning and implications of the gospel.

F. The body of Christ is a discerning body.

1. It engages in deep and intense study of what the Scriptures and the Spirit of Christ command and demand its followers to do.

2. It analyzes the sources and meaning of God's Word in terms of its original meanings and what they are saying today.

3. It is concerned about defining the nature of Christian life and obedience in contemporary terms.

G. The body of Christ is a sanctioning body.

1. It engages in admonition of its fellow members, encouraging them to live up to the vows and commitments they have made.

2. It is a disciplining body, exercising the obligation of discipline when a member fails or errs.

3. It excludes as a last resort from its membership anyone who refuses to allow himself to be *reproved* from his willful error.

The body of Christ inevitably is involved in two other functions — administration of its entire program and provision of facilities through which all its activities can take place. The above statements are an attempt, however, to describe systematically what the Christian church does.

It should be noticed that the pastor-priest role is not mentioned; neither are other roles. It is one of the author's basic assumptions that when the functional view is taken, the priest is not a prior office, but becomes merely an expediter of many of the functions mentioned. Thus, whatever specializations should be created under this perspective of the church will and should vary from one fellowship to another. Further, the massive function of transmission and interpretation of the Christian faith, which has been the sole prerogative of the religious hierarchy, is completely rejected by the perspective proposed here since, as it will be shown, the only way total ideology is avoided is by the process of group discernment.

The two functions of the above list that are especially relevant for this essay are "discerning" and "sanctioning." The basic reason for the seduction of the Christian church is that it has been engaging in a false discerning (else how could it decide that certain things are acceptable for the Christian, such as keeping slaves?) and a false admonishing (else how could a Christian continue to keep slaves after he was told it was wrong?). Obviously, the authoritarian, hierarchical process of discerning the will of God and doing it has not worked. Nor have those processes worked any better in the nonauthoritarian, nonhierarchical "democratic" groups such as congregational, Pentecostal congregations. Neither type of organization has been structured for discernment.

Rarely have Christian churches or fellowship groups seen the will of God correctly and done it. Where and when they have, the discernment and admonition functions were adequately implemented. What is required for adequate discernment and admonition? In the following condensed manner, the basic requisites that allow for a "structure for discernment" will be described.

The discernment of God's revelation and will implies a long history of interrelationships between a group of persons. That is, a perceptual grid must be established, where a common set of symbols, words, meanings, goals, and actions are available to a group of persons from which they can understand what is impinging upon them from without and from within. The development of the children of Israel, God's chosen people, illustrates such a length of human interaction which formed the matrix for the revelation of God. Hence, adequate discernment requires that Christians interact with each other over a long period of time (the length dimension) so that a common set of perceptual facilities are available.

Thus far nothing new has been required, for the traditional Christian church has a long history of interaction, totaling almost 2,000 years. This length of interaction, which constitutes one of the longest interaction systems in the history of man, has a profound significance, for it involves the talking back and forth between grandfathers and grandsons, between "clouds of witnesses" and those presently in the strife. An important fund of knowledge has accumulated, as the Roman Catholic Church well shows. But the truth must be related to the times, and hence needs continual renewal.

Nevertheless, the discernment has still been predominantly false. Why? Here the depth dimension comes in. For although the doctors of law, theologians, and priests have been part of a long tradition, their interaction with each other and with their fellow body of Christians has been very segmented and highly superficial. For a theologian or priest to determine what God's will is without intimate interaction with his fellow believers who are to accept that interpretation is patently contradicting the way in which human beings accept their basic presuppositions and commitments.

The depth of human interrelationship necessary for a correct discernment of God's will demands the following: (1) the interaction must be deep enough so that each trusts the motivation of the other persons involved in the discernment process; (2) the interaction must be deep enough so that the basic superficialities and masks are torn off and the bedrock concerns and motivations are exposed; (3) the interaction must be deep enough so that the most fundamental and significant common concerns and motivations of humanity emerge, uncontaminated by the individual idiosyncrasies of individual lives.

Clearly this type of discernment cannot take place well in the highly individualized and abstracted setting of the theologian in his academic ivory tower, nor for that matter in the councils and other "group" theologizing that the Christian church has engaged in for centuries. These groups did come up with the profoundest type of terminology, but it lacked, first, the confrontation with reality and, second, the conviction that "grass roots" participation automatically brings with it.

But human relationships in adequate length and depth still do not guarantee that discernment is being fully achieved. One

135

profound difficulty with contemporary social interaction is its segmented nature. One person relates to another these days predominantly as only a partial person. Role segregation, role
specialization, and role professionalization have developed to the
point where we are dealing only with a mask, or a mechanical
stimulus-response system, rather than with the whole man in his
entirety.

For too much of the time when Christians meet in the formal
public liturgy (which most Americans at least assume is
the sum total of "church"), it is as "worshipers" come to a
public performance, dressed and manicured so as to "put their
best foot forward." Each person has sloughed off all his other
identities, and comes to the divine service as "Mr. or Mrs.
Christian." There is little occasion (even in attempts to break
down this segregation during coffee hours) for a person to come
as a whole being: as a husband with almost impossible responsibility as a middle manager (as Mr. Manager), or with financial
obligations which he was foolish enough to incur (as Mr. Debtor),
as the father of a rebellious son (as Mr. Square Father); or
as a wife with her own ambitions and drives, but with a husband who stands between the wife and self-realization.

Discernment which does not involve the entire person in all
his roles and in all his conflicts and struggles is not discernment,
even though the relationship may have length and depth as
described above. Discernment (theologizing) can take place only
as entire persons relate to others in their entirety, so that
the gospel is actually incarnated in the breadth and complexity
of the reality of the human conditions and needs and in the
search for answers to these needs. The meaning of the gospel
can be spelled out for man if it is related to all aspects of life,
not only the institutional and the formal.

As a matter of fact, the formal aspects of religious behavior
need little discernment. Is it God's will that the Sunday school
should come before the worship hour? Should the offering pre-
cede the sermon or follow it? These are not the questions
where biblical discernment is needed; they could be decided
by children. But questions such as "What is the congregation's

136

responsibility toward poverty in the community?" or "What should be done about war taxes?" need very careful discernment and involve the entire brotherhood.

What type of group will foster the type of relationships that have been described above as being the minimum requirements for discernment? The primary group, without question, meets the requirements. What does a primary group consist of? One that meets the requisites of length, depth, and breadth! Is this the only place where discernment will be possible? Yes. What of the learned theologian and the ecclesiast? They bring technical competence and skills, but they do not have any biblical or theological monopoly in the discerning of God's will for men in every time and place.

The only problem is that primary groups rarely are found within the church structure. And when they are found, they deal with things such as planning the next Sunday night program or raising money for the budget. Primary groups generally form around activities which people do together. Hence, since church activities have consisted of planning programs or celebrating certain liturgical and seasonal events, no groups have emerged around the event or activity of discerning! When discerning once becomes an activity as serious as playing bridge or canvassing for the yearly budget, the primary group will form around that function. When a pastor asks for groups of members to wrestle with a local problem, such as the race issue, a primary group forms and discernment begins.

Why has the primary group not been prevalent as a discerning body in the Christian church? There are many reasons, not all of equal importance. For one thing, the theologizing function has historically become restricted to the professionals; the masses have been considered incapable of discernment. Again, the fear that diversity and even chaotic contradictions might be the consequences of various groups' discernment has argued for a single orthodox position (as if the various denominations and groups have produced a uniform system of beliefs!). In addition, the development of a learned clergy has tended to intimidate laymen so that they have abandoned the function entirely; technical proficiency is almost always confused with wisdom and insight. Church leaders have always felt threatened by "cell groups" within their charge, for leaders are never sure of what may develop in small group interaction.

The "structure for discernment" is the primary group. It must be the response to the process of listening to God in human life. People with like minds and concerns about race, war, poverty, human need, and witnessing to government will soon find themselves together in a face-to-face relationship, developing a feeling of comradeship and meeting in a common search for the truth. This, incidentally, is one of the classical definitions for the primary group; it also reflects the dimensions of length, depth, and breadth outlined above.

But are there not a great number of handicaps to leaving the all-important task of discernment to laymen? Is it any more than pooled ignorance? The theology of primary group decision-making cannot be expanded on here; it has been dealt with in differing ways by various experts and scholars. Suffice it to say that discernment by a learned man is still subjective unless tested by others. An encyclical, even by the pope, is still a personal, biased statement even when tested by the cardinals. The true understanding of God's will comes as the faithful gather together "all with one accord in one place." Then "suddenly there comes a sound from heaven as of a rushing mighty wind" as they test their collective faith against their experience under God's leading.

There is no more summary dispatching of all subjective hierarchical and traditional distinctions than when all are involved in making a decision. The Christian church cannot wait much longer or its chances will be gone entirely. God Himself is a God of a people and He relates to them as a people (the church, the body of Christ); so the response must be as a people since that is the way He deals with individuals. The mutual responsibility we bear for each other is the ultimate meaning of the priesthood of all believers and is the final mandate for discernment on a primary level. The priest may be responsible for my soul, but I am also responsible for his; so I am as responsible for discernment as he is.

But discernment of God's will, even when arrived at by the members of the covenant community, is not enough by itself. The human fact still remains, that man often knows what he ought to do, but he does not achieve it. The Apostle Paul, referred to earlier, illustrates the principle: "For I delight in the law of God after the inward man: but I see a different law in my members, warring against the law of my mind, and bringing me into captivity under the law of sin which is in my members" (Romans 7:22, 23). Shakespeare wrote about the "native hue of resolution" as "sicklied o'er with the pale cast of thought" (*Hamlet*, Act III, Scene 1). The annual folk ceremony of New Year's resolutions made in the face of knowledge that they may be broken before liqueur has run out has probably put the hope of achieving human goals into their proper perspective!

But, as was indicated earlier, the "children of darkness" are wiser than the "children of light." The "native hue of resolution" made when a man volunteers for the army is supported by considerable external structural support in most countries. If he leaves the unit without permission, he is AWOL and can be prosecuted. If he disobeys an order or perpetrates some other disobedience, he can be punished and ultimately court-martialed if he is incorrigible. All of these external structural supports for the man who voluntarily commits himself to the organization! The draftee is a more complicated case, and it may well be his ambiguous "taking of the step" that needs more external supports.

Society at large has learned from long experience that a man's verbal or mental subjective resolution is often not sufficient to achieve the behavior implied in the resolution. College and university matriculations provide for the voluntary pledge of the student to abide by its rules. But most colleges and universities have their own police systems, their deans of students, and other structures, to "help" students stay in line.

Probably the boldest example of this problem is the almost incredible way that politicians since time immemorial have been involved in the circumvention of laws they themselves have helped to make to control other people's behavior! Thus, a politician can vote against federal subsidies and federal aid and yet himself accept many thousands of dollars annually under many federal subsidies. To enact laws that will help curb people's tendency to fall short of their commitment, and then to flaunt those laws themselves is the epitome in cynical admission of the need for external support.

The Christian church has long faced the problem of what to do about keeping members faithful to their vows. Its success has varied greatly; the predominant result of the attempt has been dismal failure. In some cases where the Christian church has failed its mission it is not because it has not known what was right, but rather that it has not had the courage to do the right. It is impossible to examine very closely this assertion, since an enormous amount of research would be necessary. It is possible to suggest, however, that the German persecution of the Jews was something some of the German churches knew to be wrong, but did nothing about it. No doubt some members of the Reformed Church in South Africa know that what it is doing to the blacks is non-Christian, but is doing it anyhow.

Where the church has not been victim of total ideology, it has often continued to varying degrees in a practice which it knew to be wrong. How can this be explained? Very simply, because of the lack of mechanisms whereby a covenantal promise was not backed up with structural supports. The Christian church has allowed its members to make fantastic verbal confessions and commitments without a shred of structure to back them up. Only in a religious ceremonial event can a man get up and "move mountains" verbally and be lauded for his beautiful performance without a momentary thought about the "reality" of that verbal torrent. In the world of science, a man makes a statement and backs it up with facts, or he is laughed out of court. In the church, the more bizarre a person's verbal promises and accomplishments, the more he is honored without any reflection on whether there is any relationship between his verbal behavior and his life. As Peter

140

Berger has so well epitomized it, the church is literally the "Noise of Solemn Assemblies."

What is required for the church to become "free" as it has been defined above? It will be free when its yea will be yea and its nay, nay. That is to say, when the Christian family can make a confession and say "Jesus is Lord," and then go and live under Jesus as Lord, then the Christian church will be a "free" church, both in terms of its understanding of God and of itself, and in terms of its freedom to do it. "Blessed are they that hear [discern] the word of God, and do it" (Luke 11:28) is one of the most profound and simple commandments ever produced by any religion, and Christianity is its author.

Historically, from time to time the Christian church has seen attempts to respond to the call to do as well as hear. Many of the Catholic monastic orders were attempts at living the more "narrow" way of the cross, or at following Jesus. The Reformation produced attempts such as the Anabaptist church discipline, with the ban as the final act reserved for the totally unrepentant. But even before the Anabaptists the Hussites in Bohemia protested the degeneracy of the Roman Catholic Church and demanded "moral reform rather than ecclesiastical revolution."[10] The "class meeting" instituted by John Wesley is probably the most notable of recent attempts at marrying confession to life. That Methodist class societies could issue "tickets" indicating that each member was in good standing and had lived up to his commitments indicates that here was an attempt to "structure" the consequence of verbal and subjective confession.

Unfortunately, the "class meeting" and other attempts at structuring the response to commitment have not survived. It is not possible to analyze why these attempts failed. In any case it can be said that the disappearance of the structured support, the accounting for Christian profession, has gone by the board. The principle of the "structure of accountability" has been correct, even though the application may not have been. The Anabaptist stress on excommunication and ban for unrepentant sinning may have been the wrong approach, but its purpose was

141

correct. What method or technique as yet untried can achieve the "structure of accountability" which we have said is absolutely imperative in principle?

The method-technique which has not yet been tried is the peer group — "koinonia group," in theological language! One of the most powerful forces in human society is peer group conformity. An enormous amount of research has proved the strength of conformity and cohesion to peer group values. Study of adolescence shows that peers are more powerful than parents or other authority figures. Academic peers are the only people that really matter as far as scholars are concerned. There is even a respect for norms among gangs and gang members, for if one disobeys, he walks the plank. The church has been ambivalent toward peer groups, and has in fact often discouraged them. But where a group of Christians is engaged in living together and consider this group *the* group to belong to, a peer force (koinonia) is operative. When a Christian wants to relate to a group of other Christians, the basic dynamic achieving "structure for accountability" has been satisfied.

Once a Christian desires to be with others who are similar in many respects, he is willing to submit himself to their scrutiny and judgment. He is willing to reveal some of his frustrations and failures and to allow the group to help him. In fact, the peer (koinonia) group knows all about him, and knows what type of profession he has made and how well he is achieving it. No judgment is as important to him as the judgment of his peers. This applies to all peer group relationships; it could and does apply as well to Christians. A minister is more worried about the judgment of other ministers than about any laymen, as witness a ministerial conference where most of the time is spent in trying to impress peers with the orthodoxy and achievements of each.

Why has the Christian church not encouraged peer or koinonia groups as the natural "structure for accountability"? Again this cannot be adequately dealt with here, but a number of rather obvious reasons emerge; (1) the minister-priest has always been threatened by any activity in his parish or congregation which was not directly under his control, and peer groups imply — in fact, demand — this very thing; (2) the theology of the Christian church has traditionally looked with disfavor upon lay activity, whether it be deciding how a service should be run or the "holy" act of theologizing; (3) the structure of religious institutions has made the peer group rather difficult to realize. With the great sanctity of the sacerdotal function of the Sunday morning worship hour, any religious activity which does not include the entire congregation or parish in its public institutional character has been considered sectarian and heretical. (The Sunday school movement could well have become a healthy counterforce, but it got bogged down in pedantic scholasticism, from which it apparently will never recover.); (4) the societal structure has made peer group (koinonia) formation among Christians very difficult because of the way community has become fragmented. Now it is easier for peers at the job, at school, or in the community to get together than it is for peer Christians! Many people literally admit that it is easier and more natural to relate to noncovenant members in a peer setting than to their own covenant peers. This has its good side for evangelism, but its other function, the structuring for accountable living, has gone by the board.

If the peer (koinonia) group is the solution to helping Christians live like Christians, then how can such groups be launched? Several things must take place: (1) the congregation or denomination must recognize the theological and ecclesiastical significance of peer (koinonia) groups and stress this to the membership; (2) the membership must be helped to organize the peer (koinonia) groups, not through arbitrary means, but through the guidance of the Holy Spirit and the natural workings of human choices, feelings, and fears; (3) the peer groups must be given or must possess sufficient biblical and theological understanding so that they can develop peer group standards which are consistent with the biblical tradition. This latter point ties in with the discerning function discussed above and needs no further analysis here.

The "peer group" concept may strike many Christians as

negative and even non-Christian, for is not the Christian to be ignorant of class distinctions and to regard everyone as his peer? Does the peer group concept not exclude the old from a group with predominantly young? Does it not exclude the rich from the group which has poor in it? Isn't the peer group the most smug, monolithic, and ethnocentric structure imaginable? A secular peer group, yes; but not a Christian group! A Christian peer (koinonia) group is that group of Christians who have in common the important values, goals, and commitments — the group who means most to me in terms of my Christian commitments. This can — in fact, often does — cut across all status distinctions of age, education, wealth, culture, and experience.

A peer group carries its own authenticity and accreditation and attraction. If it operates in secular life, it can operate in the church. But until now it has not been allowed to express its true potential. Where peer (koinonia) groups of Christians have developed, they have aroused great interest and others have "wanted in," which has resulted in the formation of more groups. Once begun, they take over the functions that must be performed if the Christian church is to recapture her leadership. This is a personal observation of the author, after participating in five "koinonia" groups in fifteen years.

The way the Holy Scripture finally became collected into a canon makes a fitting conclusion. Even though scholars and theologians and councils deliberated and evaluated them, it was the dynamics of the Word among the people that determined the canon.

> The councils simply made official what the church had already accepted and had been using. . . . What the councils did was to ratify the spiritual insight of the rank and file of the church. It is not true that any convocation of bishops forced the Bible on the church — made them swallow it, as it were. On the contrary, the church — the great mass of Christians — without pressure from priests or bishops had already found these books to contain spiritual food.[11]

History reveals many ironies. One of them is that a holy canon which emerged out of the experience of numerous lay peer groups in day-by-day struggle has later become something that laymen could not understand nor be trusted with!

8

The Dimensions of
the Divine Order

After so much discussion, what are some specific social structures which pertain to the achievement of the discernment and admonition? It may appear odd to talk about the value of structures when the general mood in our world is increasingly antistructure. But any realistic and sober perspective will conclude that human life without form is as dead as form without life; hence it is important to understand what structures do to the cognitive process and how these same structures can be used in a positive way.

1. The Large Gathering

Let us begin by asking what role the large gathering plays in the discernment and admonition function. Directly, the large gathering has very little to offer; indirectly, it may have more. But before going farther, let us propose an arbitrary definition for "large gathering" as consisting of more than twenty-five persons. The rationale for this distinction will be spelled out later. At this point we need to accept the basis for the distinction — namely, that in a group of over twenty-five persons interaction is predominantly a one-way process, emanating from one person and directed toward the rest.[1]

Clearly, the large group is useful only for certain functions. The amount of time that a large group normally meets together is probably less than two hours, although in earlier days large groups met for much longer periods of time. The average length of religious large-group meetings may be about 1 1/2 hours. If the interaction is to have any type of order, it will need to originate with one person. Several types of interaction are possible: 1. The "formal classroom" type. In this type, the leader is the dispenser of the ideas, suggestions, or directions for behavior, and the "students" merely do what they are told. 2. The news conference type. In this type, all of the interaction is focused on one person, although the action may emanate from any person to all others in turn. The "informer" or newsgiver is the hub of activity and its controller. 3. The business meeting type. Here the interaction can be initiated by anyone, but it is controlled by a person authorized to achieve the objectives of the meeting. The interaction, however, is not normally directed to individuals but rather to the entire group.

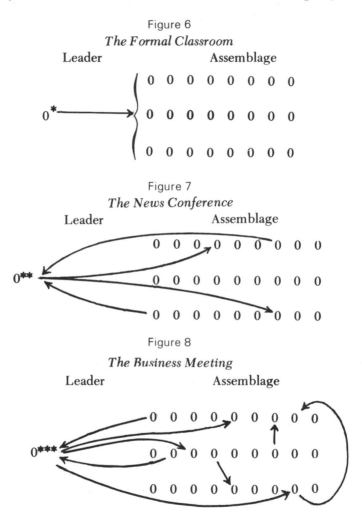

Figure 6
The Formal Classroom

Leader   Assemblage

Figure 7
The News Conference

Leader   Assemblage

Figure 8
The Business Meeting

Leader   Assemblage

°leader initiates and directs behavior.
°°leader responds to initiation, but controls all behavior.
°°°leaders initiate and receive behaviors, but control pattern of meeting.

148

There are limitations of the large gathering in its varying types. If the meeting is an hour long, each person theoretically has four minutes of time allotted to him under types two and three, assuming that there are no formalities and no monopolizers, which is rare. Under type one, each person has exactly no time for any initiation unless the leader grants it. Notice further that in order for there to be any semblance of order, the interaction must be channeled through a "gatekeeper," for as soon as simultaneous interaction begins, chaos takes over, as any schoolteacher knows too well.

Finally, it is almost imperative that the interaction be directed toward an individual as a representative of the entire group, for any type of individual or personal interaction immediately impinges on other people's time and creates an immediate threat for breakdown of the group. A person dare not express any personal needs or interests, for that breaks down the cohesion of the group's existence.

These basic facts suggest that the size of the group beyond the arbitrary limit of 25 makes very little difference. Whether the group consists of 27 or 270, very little has changed in the basic structure or function of the group. As a matter of fact, the size could be 2,700 without changing the basic form.

What is a group of over 25 people good for? Speaking in the context of our description of the functions of the church, groups of over 25 are useful for the church in the function of worship, the function of teaching, and the function of serving, if serving is assumed to include the problem of the organization and facilitation of people to do the serving on a mass basis. Social worship can be conducted with a mass of any size, for it involves leading of people in collective behavior (at least the objective aspects). Teaching, insofar as it is the transmission of information, can also be conducted on any scale. Where expertise is involved, a class on the history of the denomination can as easily be composed of 200 people as 20.

By its very nature, the large gathering cannot be convoked very often, for it is impossible to find a time when all can meet for an extended period of time unless it is thoroughly

149

institutionalized. That is to say, unless the place, time, and format of a large gathering is set well in advance, specifically organized, very definite in terms of time for beginning and ending and being specific in terms of the content of the meeting and of what will be the requirements for participation, good attendance and participation will be lacking. Hence, the large gathering is usually a periodic one, usually on Sunday morning, usually at a specific time. This type of gathering tends to support the length aspect of human interaction if members participate faithfully. Such a format is clearly less than useful for the breadth and depth dimensions discussed in the last chapter.

The large meeting as an institutionalized structure, therefore, provides opportunity for a corporate witness to how God has led, which becomes praise. It serves as an opportunity for corporate prayer and thanksgiving and reaffirmation through all the cultural forms that have developed for that purpose, namely, singing, praying, commemoration services, and the like. The large meeting also offers real possibilities for teaching. In this setting, the trained technical experts in theology, history, ethics, and sociology can instruct the participants in what their tradition means, what has been considered right behavior, and what the context is in which their life is being lived.

Serving the world is also a major function of the large group in that both the education on world needs and the response to it are in part that of large gatherings. In these larger groups information is dispensed, and responses are made which have the benefit of group or crowd psychology. The secular use of large political rallies has its religious counterpart and does not need to be discounted or disparaged. It is often in the fellowship of others that one is brought to make a commitment that one ought to have made, but did not in the individualness of one's own existence. The organization of personal resources, physical resources, and other things is often best expedited in large meetings where those with a common orientation meet for a common purpose.

The large group is thus a gathering in which there is a long tradition of interaction, which helps to establish an orientation from which reality is perceived, but it is not able to fulfill many other functions. It is premised on a one-way type of interaction, namely, a response to an initiative. The interaction is thus that of a group and its leader, rather than interaction of members of a group with each other. This is the cardinal difference which distinguishes this form of structure from the one which will now be discussed.

2. The Small Gathering

It was suggested above that an arbitrary number of 25 separated the large group from the small. The basic variable was the type of interaction — that of a group with its leader, or that of members of a group with each other. The theoretical basis for this arbitrary distinction or delineation will now be expanded. Almost everyone is aware that it is easier to participate in a small group than a large one. In fact, it is probably true that most of us have developed some rule of thumb about the maximum size of group in which all of the members of the group can participate. What we lack is merely the scientific specification of the variable involved.

In order to advance the discussion, some arbitrary limitations will need to be set, but they will affect the general applicability only to the degree that they appreciably change the nature of the factors. Let us assume that the group in question is composed of 14 people, that it meets once a week, and that it meets for about two hours. On this basis, there will be 98 different interactions possible, based on the formula $X = \dfrac{Y^2 - Y}{2}$

where X is the number of pairs of relationships possible, Y is the number of persons in the meeting. That is to say, there are 98 different combinations of individuals possible in a group of 14 persons. If we would insist that each person should interact with every other person, in the above group it would allow each combination to interact for slightly more than one minute while the others listened!

However, in a group which is not focusing on any particular topic, more opportunity is offered for interaction. In a group of 14, it is possible for seven of the possible 98 combinations of interaction to take place at one time. Thus in a two-hour meeting, each combination of two persons would be able to interact about nine minutes. But a random "group" which has no central focus, but is engaged in random interaction is not achieving any task aside from purely socio-emotional gratification. There is no point in downgrading socio-emotional interaction, but the present discussion assumes a purpose for the small group.

It is clear that a "collectivity" of 14 persons which engages in the random interaction described above is not very useful. Each person should be able to contribute to the group's process, and should be given the opportunity to do so if the group is to have an objective and move toward its achievement. Hence, it is impossible that each person in a small group will be able to respond individually to each other person's contribution, as was indicated above, nor can the pairs of interaction take place simultaneously. The only reasonable alternative thus is for each individual to be given opportunity to interact with the others in the group as though the group were an individual. Therefore, in a group of 14 members, each person should theoretically have nine minutes of interaction time with the other person (the entire group). If the average unit of interaction takes 30 seconds, each person will be able to initiate 18 units of interaction in an evening meeting.

Let us assume that one eighth of the 18 units of interaction are classed as question units (trying to gain information) and the other seven eighths are answer units (giving information or stating opinion).[2] Adding the group's totals, we would have about 35 questioning inputs and 217 statements of opinion. This kind of exchange offers considerable data for gaining information and for gaining orientation. However, it should be noted that the figures and conclusions arrived at here are based on theoretical factors, and that any actual group may deviate considerably from this profile.

When comparing the profile of interaction possible in a small group as compared to a large group, it is immediately obvious that some significant differences, especially for our purposes, emerge. First, and most important, the units of interaction can be initiated by any member of the group, although there will probably never be an equal participation by all members. Second, the amount of interaction initiated by any member will be considerably higher than in a large group. Third, each person can relate to others in the group and address individuals or the entire group as his object of interaction, and there is a potentially possible feedback from each other (or the entire group seen as a person) to the person initiating the interaction. The types of interactions possible are illustrated in the following diagrams.

Figure 9

Random Interaction°

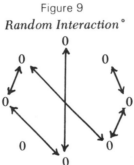

°Only a few of the 91 possible combinations are shown in order not to clutter the figure.

Figure 10

Individual-Group Interaction

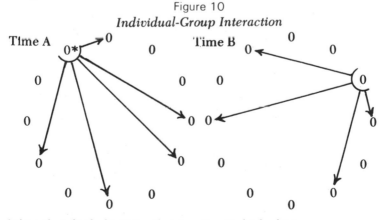

°This is the individual initiating the interaction. Each takes his turn.

153

Figure 11
A Combination Random and Individual-Group °

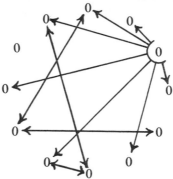

°Only a few of the possible random and individual-group interactions are pictured in order not to clutter the diagram too much.

Finally, the small group allows for a combination of various types of interaction, which is not possible in a large group. For example, if one member wants to address the group or an individual, he can do so without hindering some small person-to-person groups from taking place, which contributes to the progress of the group's work. In other words, the small group can do what the large group can do, in addition to allowing for individual interactions.

The small group has been studied rather comprehensively in terms of its performance and functions, but little has been stated of a normative nature that indicates what small groups are good for. Of course, as indicated earlier, it was the concern of many leading sociological thinkers that the concept of community was in danger of being lost through the permeation of society by secondary and contractual relationships. Hence, the primary group, a small group, is important for the fabric of society at large. But it is even more important for the achievement of the objectives of the Christian gospel, as was indicated above, through the depth and breadth dimensions of the Christian life.

But how does the small group, the primary group, figure in our analysis of the central functions of the Christian church

154

discussed above? What special properties does it possess which make it vital for the church's life? First of all, it can perform more of the functions of the life of the church than the larger group can. In other words, the small group can do what the large group can do, and it can do some things that the large group can't do. It has most of the assets of the large group and few if any of its liabilities.

To run down the list, the small group can participate in the worship and fellowship acts of the Christian church. There is no reason why a small group can't engage in praise, prayer, song, and other symbolic expressions as well as a large group. In fact, many of the more creative worship patterns are emerging in small group experiments. The small group can also engage in witnessing, in confessing the lordship of Christ, and in preaching and prophesying as effectively as the larger congregation, for all individual acts of witnessing are as effectively done when encouraged by the small group as by the larger fellowship. In fact, the encouragement and identification which can be achieved in small group sharing can be more effective than in a large group.

The small group can be a reconciling body to a much better degree than can the large group. Forgiving, restoring, and forbearing are almost by definition acts that involve direct confrontation of individuals, which is rarely effectively accomplished in large groups. The acts of forgiveness described in the New Testament almost invariably refer to forgiveness in the context of two or three gathered. This is not to say that reconciliation of an individual in a larger congregational group is not possible, but simply to say that it is not as easily and naturally achieved.

The small group can be a serving body in all the respects that a larger body can. A family in need can as easily be brought into the bosom of the church through the ministries of a small group dedicated to service as through a large group. The small group is limited, however, in engaging in any type of service which demands resources beyond the command of the small group. But then the congregation is in many ways just as incapable of meeting the needs of the larger community, such as housing, or of the world, such as war relief.

The teaching functions of the small group are probably not as effective as the larger group, for competence and efficiency usually demand larger numbers. A Sunday school program that takes care of 100 children is as good as a small number — maybe better — and will probably have better trained personnel and better resources. But the small group can in an informal and unstructured way teach its own members through the normal interaction patterns in its life. Thus a small group can, if there are some knowledgeable persons in it, become informed about its own religious tradition and heritage as well as the larger group.

It is, however, in the discerning and sanctioning functions that the small group becomes paramount and central in the purposes of our discussion. It has been stated numerous times above that the reason for the failure of the Christian church to be the church is that it has become seduced by its environment. The discussion has maintained that the central issue is a self-awareness of egocentricity and ethnocentricity. How does the small group fit into this function? The central issue is confrontation. The transition from a primary to a secondary type of societal relationship has allowed for the individual to become anonymous; that is, he is accountable to no one.

On the other hand, the primary group is premised on the process of confrontation by definition! For example, the intimate friendship of three persons almost automatically precludes any amount of avoidance of openness and sharing. The best example, of course, is the married couple, where any attempt to hide and evade confrontation is clearly headed for dissolution. A primary group can survive only if its members are willing to submit themselves to mutual examination and responsibility.

The absence of confrontation is precisely what allows for a man with all the appearances of respectability and honesty to be found guilty of embezzlement. It allows for the politician to make one type of promise to his constituency and another type to himself. It allows for the businessman to produce shoddy merchandise and pawn it off on the public for a long time before someone finally is able to confront him with his behavior. The lack of personal confrontation in the secular world is to a considerable degree responsible for the great gap between the public morality as officially stated and actually achieved. But in the Christian church the lack of confrontation is a much more serious thing. The gospel of Christ is premised on the position that it is of no avail to hear or know what is demanded, if it is not lived. "A man is justified before God by what he does as well as what he believes."[3] But, as has been demonstrated above, the Christian church has been guilty of a monstrous hypocrisy.

The primary group in the Christian congregation takes the objective aspects of the Christian faith and makes them operate in the individual life. Hence the individual's expressions of joy, thankfulness, commitments, and service are brought into a social context where what a person says and what he does are not allowed to diverge. In the large group, public and ceremonial religious behavior is easily enacted, but the consequences or implications of the ritual are left hanging unless an intimate group that knows about the person is willing to check out his behavior.

In the discernment process, confrontation is crucial since it helps prevent personal, subjective, idiosyncratic, bizarre, deceptive, and all other "unsanctified" motives from taking precedence over the objective import of the gospel intent. It is possible that even theologians can become victims of self-deceit unless confronted by others. Now of course the confrontation of the peer group through the process of scientific criticism and scrutiny ultimately forces a theologian's thinking off the shelves and into the nether regions of heresy or poppycock if indeed it is such, but the theologian as a person himself rarely is subjected to the moral obligations that even his writings entail! Were each theologian to test his theologizing with a small primary group of fellow Christians, much irresponsible thinking would be avoided.

The same goes for preaching. Where feedback is tried, even

in a larger audience, the words of proclamation are often restrained and made more responsible. Where a minister periodically allows his preaching to be confronted by members of his congregation, there is more responsible preaching and more responsible response. Horst Symanowski, in one of the most creative industrial ministries now operating, meets weekly with a group of his co-workers at a plant where he works.[4] The honest, brutal exchange that takes place chastens the proclamation and makes it more authentic.

But in determining what God's word is for us today, the most significant and sacred moment in religious life is encountered. There is here no room for the unrestrained and personalized perceptions to enter it. All the wisdom, as well as the technical knowledge, available in the larger congregation must be used in order to perceive the voice of God. The small group does not allow human selfishness to intervene. The personal and direct confrontation of the primary group makes careful discernment an achievable goal. It has never been achieved outside the small group, and cannot, if the argument above is correct.

3. Confrontation

We have said that the small group is the key to adequate discernment and sanctioning, without which the church becomes seduced by its environment. We have indicated that the small group provides for confrontation, which is the critical variable. Let us look a little more closely at the concept of confrontation as it relates to our thesis and indicate why it is more effective in avoiding ideology than is a large group.

Our discussion has assumed that individuals are egotists, self-seeking and self-deceiving. It has also intimated that large groups are no better, for they can become the opportunity for exploitation or misleading by clever leaders, or they can become so institutionalized that no meaningful interaction takes place at all. Since both mass movements and individuals are prone to become victims of various moods and false ideologies, there must be some structure that protects the individual from this tyranny. We have said it is the small group. Why is this so?

In the first place, in the small group each individual has a status. That is to say, in a group of 14 people each individual has a status which is recognized by everyone else. If A is not present, members B through N are aware of the fact that A's status is not filled. Each member is cognizant of the missing person and feels the loss in the group's totality and completeness. There are a number of consequences or corollaries of this fact. Some of the sociological concerns mentioned in chapter two are obviously served in this structure. For example, alienation, the need for community, is spoken to in this situation. In a group where each person "counts," alienation is not nearly as prone to develop as where each member belongs to no group. There is also a natural effort to keep the cohesion of the group intact and to preserve its life. Hence, any "dropouts" are carefully nurtured to remain in the group and to relate to others. This does not take place in a large group — not even in a congregation. Where a "group spirit" develops, each individual begins to discover his importance in the life of the group and becomes more active in it. In addition, each person begins to fulfill his role as a supporter of the cohesion of the group. That is to say, each person begins to discover in practice that he is responsible to help each other person remain faithful to the group and support it. The motivation is obvious: if each member counts, then each person will do his part to see that each other member will show up. A very good example of the principle that each has a status is to observe a group of boys trying to maintain a baseball club. It is to the advantage of each that every member appear for practice and for games.

Second, every member of the group recognizes that each member has a function as well as a status. In contrast to the large group, in the small group not only does each person have a status, but also has a function. Small group research has shown conclusively how significant each person's functions are, and how they in fact develop. Individual differences, interests, and finally gifts are clearly delineated in a small group, as well as encouraged. Hence, in a small group each contributes what

159

he already has, and each is strengthened and encouraged in any latent gifts he possesses.

The consequences for the discernment and sanctioning process are so obvious as to need hardly any explication at all. If discernment and sanctioning need the application of gifts, then here is the place for that to develop. If the individual differences and concerns as well as problems receive their expression in a small group, then it is obvious how sanctioning for example needs to take place here, for here is where the individual's uniqueness comes out into the open so that it can be dealt with.

Third, the small group demands the strictest adherence to the norms by which it operates. Each member is aware of the norms that are in effect in the group, and each person is strongly expected and encouraged to operate by these norms. He is offered no excuse by way of ignorance, weakness, or other rationalization. If he has joined the group, by whatever formal or informal means that takes place, he has committed himself to those norms, and he must abide by them or get out. The normative behavior is strong because the individuals participate in the creation of these norms and in their preservation. This is again a great difference from the large group, where the norms are usually traditional norms, and where the enforcement has been formalized and objectivized so that deviation is spelled out in legalistic ways with no personal confrontation of individual and deviance.

The consequences for discernment and sanctioning again are very clear. If a member himself contributes to the norms (beliefs, ideals, attitudes, values), it is clear that he will be more vitally interested in them and contribute to their survival and viability. If he has helped make them, he will be more concerned that they are obeyed, not in a legalistic or formal way, but in the spirit in which they were created. He will also be concerned about other members of the group and their submission to the norms, for he knows that the norms, as well as the very group's future, depend upon the protection of the norms and their authority over the members of the group. The problem of authority, discussed in chapter two, is squarely spoken to in this dimension, for in the small group the personal subjection to an objective norm and the individual's concern about others' subjection are fortunately joined, so that each contributes to the other's concern for norms and others' support of the norms. There is here no need for some to "lord it over others."

Fourth, because members of a small group normally live in proximity their lives intersect at many points other than the small group meeting. In fact, the small group's formal meetings are often the least significant of its relationships. It is in the normal day-by-day contacts that the opportunities present themselves for the deepening of the relationship, and for the reinforcement of the membership in the small group and all the requirements that this entails. Hence, what a person does or says in the small group is cross-tabulated with what he does outside it. Thus, the private and public life of the small group member is much more closely allied than that of the member of a large group.

The consequences for the sanctioning process are obvious. If a person's actions need "policing," the only place this can be done is where each person is responsible for a "buddy." Otherwise, the social structure would collapse. It is impossible to have as many policemen as there are people unless it is an informal system described above. Hence, sanctioning in the Christian life can take place only where this type of structure is present. The consequences for the social structure are also significant. Only if each is concerned about his own behavior and that of his neighbor will a public morality emerge which will create order. The collective conscience must be enforced by everyone if it is to emerge at all.

4. The Structuring of Small Groups in Christian Congregations

Many people in the Christian church need no convincing that the small group is a very important requirement for the survival of the church as it exists today, not to mention the hope for its release from ideology. But how can the local congregation encourage or achieve small group participation? Many congregations have attempted to achieve small group life, but have failed for many reasons. A recounting of some of the reasons may help to answer the question.

Small groups are difficult to develop in congregations for a number of reasons, the main one probably being that of tradition. The institutionalized public ceremonial known as the Sunday morning worship service has become so deeply embedded in Christendom as the religious event that nothing else seems important. Hence, any attempt to suggest the need for other experiences or activities falls on deaf ears. Sunday morning church attendance has become the sign, measure, and extent of religion for many Christians. Hence, if a person is faithful in attendance (whether he sleeps through the preaching or not is beside the point), there is nothing further that could interest him. He has brought his offering to the deity and can thereafter return to his tribal pursuits. There is ample documentation in sociological research that religion can be measured only on gross measures such as church attendance, and not in behavioral differences.

Where tradition is not strong enough to hinder small group formation, the minister usually is. One of the main supporters of the traditionalized Sunday worship as the religious event is the minister, since the public mass gathering focuses and emphasizes the priestly significance and role of the minister. Thus, why should he downgrade his own significance? Many a minister is threatened by the formation within his congregation of any small groups which are not a part of the official formal structure. One of the main reasons is that he is not directly in charge of these groups and hence cannot control them. Another reason is that there is no direct means for checking up on what is going on, and it is easily possible that some ideas and attitudes might develop which would tend to undermine the minister's authority or leadership.

A third resistance factor to the formation of small groups is the people in the congregation. The presence of small groups which have formed spontaneously tends to threaten those who are not in the groups. The formation of a group immediately raises the question of inclusion-exclusion. Why was so and so included while I was excluded? This question raises the problem of distrust and suspicion about the motives and purposes of the people who have formed a small group. The remonstrance that anyone is free to form his own group does not do enough to allay the suspicion and distrust.

Even if there is no personal threat involved in not participating in small groups, often a philosophical objection is raised. That is, often people will resist the formation or joining of a small group by maintaining that small groups are divisive and detrimental to the life of the larger congregation. It is alleged that small groups allow for gossip, rumor, personal gripes, and other schismatic dynamics to emerge. Hence, it is better for everyone to simply participate in all of the public and collective activities so that all tendencies for division and schism are avoided. That this is a weak if not totally false argument does not deter those who hold this view.

A final although weaker argument is that there is enough going on already in the life of the congregation so that any more activity is unwelcome and burdensome. With all the programs, meetings, and work needed to keep things going, it is simply asking too much to participate in one more activity. Typically the argument that the small group meeting is completely different in kind does not alter such resistance.

The responses to these arguments will serve as the means to suggest how small groups (K groups in normal parlance) can be introduced into the typical congregation.

1. The resistance of traditionalism can be answered on two levels. The first is that many congregations are slowly becoming aware that they will need to change if they are to survive. For this type of congregation, the introduction of a small group structure may come easily. Typically the pastor and some more active members of the congregation have already seen the light and are leading the movement toward experimentation. This movement is especially assisted with all the material that is being published on congregational renewal.

The answer on the second level is more difficult, and refers to a congregation that is not ready to change and sees no need to. In those congregations where the pastor is sympathetic, a few experimental small groups can be organized, which may prove their value. If the pastor is not open to the movement, a small group may need to take the risk of getting started, but should be sure to keep the pastor informed. He needs to be invited often enough so that he knows what is going on, but seldom enough not to break up the integrity of the group. The important variable is communication. The congregation must be publicly informed as to what is happening and why. Usually a congregation has enough tolerance and maturity to support new experimentation.

2. Where the minister himself is the main hindrance, several observations are again in order. The first is that a minister that hinders experimentation and development in a congregation ought to be asked either to shape up or ship out. What actually happens where the minister is resistant depends upon the type of congregational-denominational structure. In a strictly congregational type of government the pastor is supposedly at the mercy of the congregation. In other forms he is more dependent upon more hierarchical structures. Even in these there are ways to move him.

But typically the minister is not openly hostile; he is merely not convinced that the K group is that important. If this is the case, he needs to be convinced of the importance of the K group, and shown that small groups do not hinder his work nor that of Christ. The best way to convince him is to show him an actual group in action. As indicated above, when a small group has been functioning and has shown its utility, the pastor is quickly convinced of its importance. The procedure should involve informing the pastor of the intention of forming a group, what its purposes are, and how it will fit into the overall structure and life of the local congregation. He should be assured that he will be kept informed and that he is welcome to attend whenever he cares to. In order to alleviate any timidity in visiting the group, he should be given some specific invitations to attend the group.

3. When the members of the congregation are the major resistance to the formation of K groups, it is important that the pastor be convinced of the group's value, for then he can interpret the activities and educate the congregation on the functions of small groups. Hence, any apprehension on the part of members can be allayed through interpretative sermons or personal discussion. Beyond this, it is important that an open and public statement or interpretation be made of the K group program, so that it does not appear as a sinister plot to destroy the congregation. Some type of evening program where the K group idea is presented and actual activities described helps to dissipate much of the anxiety.

Another useful practice is to invite members who are apprehensive about K groups to visit your group, so that they can see what actually goes on and that there is nothing subversive about them. They will note the prayers of concern for the pastor, members of the congregation and its life, and will notice the openness and sincerity of the members of the K group. This often is all the convincing that is required. Often it is possible that members of K groups have friends among those who are not convinced and are able to dispense their fears.

4. The philosophical objection that K groups are divisive and detrimental is not easily answered. For it is difficult to disallow something that has no chance of being proved or disproved. Hence, the only way to counter this argument is to ask for the privilege of proving that it is not detrimental but, rather, helpful to the life of the congregation. For this agreement to be achieved, it is important again to educate the membership on the role of small groups, and to ask for the opportunity to demonstrate their utility. After some experience, a public meeting can be arranged and the life of the small group can be described, as well as what it has done. Normally, however, this is not necessary, for the utility of the small group has long since been communicated through the informal channels of communication.

5. The final argument that there is already too much going on is the weakest argument, although maybe the most convincing one. There is too much going on, and a person could

spend all of his time in religious activities. It needs to be pointed out to the congregation that many of the activities are just busywork, and could be exchanged for something more meaningful. It also should be stressed that the K group takes the place of a lot of meaningless activity, and thus deserves as much commitment as the public worship service. Hence, it would not be out of line to suggest that the K group meeting should be considered an equivalent of attending a Sunday evening worship service or any midweek service. When this is understood and agreed to by the congregation, the argument vanishes in thin air. But it is clear that the congregation must be ready to see their activities in a new and creative way. And this goes back to the first point, the awareness of need for renewal.

Because K groups must be formed as a response to the need for them, it is very inadvisable to attempt to get them started in a utilitarian fashion. Where this has been tried, either by the pastor or by interested individuals, the consequences have been rather unhappy. K groups must form naturally and be the response to the work of the Holy Spirit and individual conscience. The development of the primary group cannot be manipulated; its development can only be encouraged. The "talking up" of the small group idea is really all that is necessary, for where an adequate understanding exists of the needs for the renewal of the Christian faith, people are usually willing to respond with the appropriate measures.

It is impossible to lay down all of the ground rules for the shape of the K groups, since each circumstance will be different. But the following rules of thumb, based on past experience, appear useful. Husbands and wives must be partners in the groups; it is dysfunctional to have husbands and wives separated in a task which involves a basic understanding of the most primary group of all, namely, the married couple. There should be some variation in the professional and vocational roles of the persons in the group. Thus, professionals such as medical doctors should be in groups with teachers and technicians. Too much variation, however, may be a hindrance, although there is no theological reason for separating the manual laborer from the president of a corporation. This would require some skill, and where such skill is available, a wide gamut of professional statuses should be encouraged.

Frequency of meeting is often a problematic concern. The author's personal preference is one meeting each week, and certainly two meetings a month is the absolute minimum. The more frequent the meetings, the more the dynamics discussed above are allowed to operate. There is little danger of too frequent meetings, for the group will naturally interlace its meetings with joviality and levity in order to preserve the easy-goingness necessary to avoid overemphasis on the task. If the K group is considered important at all, it will easily supersede another church meeting which has less meaning. If the meetings take place less frequently than twice a month, very little progress is made in the discernment and sanctioning functions, since most of the time is required to keep each other up-to-date regarding what has happened in the interval — a vital step for preserving primary relationships.

The number 14 was used earlier in the discussions of the small group size. This is a reflection of the author's own preference. If all are married, this means seven couples; or if several are single people, five or six couples and the single people. This seems to be a happy size for a number of reasons. Usually one couple is absent, and six couples are enough to preserve the identity of the group. Often in discussion a coalition is avoided when there are enough persons on a side to allow for lively discussion to bring out the full issue and assist in its resolution. In groups much smaller, too much emotional investment is borne by single individuals or couples to allow for open discussion. A group much larger than 14 begins to rapidly depress its functions and thus to mitigate against its very purpose.

The introduction of the K group into the life of the congregation is tantamount to a proposal for complete renewal in the congregation and in the church. That is to say, if the small group is introduced into the congregation, it will not only restructure the entire value system, behavior patterns, organizational structure, but it will also have as a consequence the entire change of the thought form and content in the future. For it will bring the individual into direct confrontation with the claims of the gospel, and with those others who have committed themselves to the same way.

It is not exaggeration to say that the contemporary Christian religious practice is, for all practical purposes, the same as attendance at a Fourth of July celebration or a Memorial Day parade: A public ceremony is conducted; there are many people in attendance; ritualistic lip service is paid to a host of high-sounding, but poorly understood ideals and values; individuals participate to the degree they feel inclined at the moment; and the symbolic and experiential meanings of the event have no implications for later life, for the persons who participate will continue exploiting their neighbors, denying freedom to minority groups, and so on.

Just as the Fourth of July celebration or Memorial Day parade is more a rationalization for what is than what ought to be, so the sacred Christian rituals are more rationalizations for what is than submissions to a transcendental God who demands obedience to His will. It is clear that a thousand years of celebrating the Fourth of July would never have brought about the civil rights revolution and at least the beginnings of the human freedoms so loudly championed in all national ceremonies. It is equally clear that two thousand years of Christian ritualistic celebration has not brought Christians one step closer to being representatives of the Christ they trumpet about. Among Christians war is no less plausible, poverty is still due to indolence and depravity, and the strong still dominate the weak. There is no hope for the church short of a birth of conscience that acknowledges that the Christian faith has been prostituted. This can come about only with the practice of discernment and confrontation, as described in this book.

The curse of Christianity is the Christian who can pledge allegiance to the Christ and totally disregard His teachings and His life. How is this possible? How can a man pray the Lord's

Prayer and support war? How can a man listen to the story of the rich man and Lazarus and discriminate against the poor by charging more interest of them than of his "best borrowers"? He can do these things and many more simply because he doesn't "see" his hypocrisy and because he can get by with them!

The curse of the Christian church as evidenced in the local congregation is that a member can live as he pleases and still be a part of the "Fourth of July celebration." In the historic peace churches it is possible for a person to belong to the "club" and not to subscribe to the biblical teachings on peace. It is possible for a man to belong to a Lutheran congregation and still not believe in the holiness of God. It is possible to belong to a Pentecostal Holiness group and get by with adultery. Why? Because the "Fourth of July" is for everybody, on whatever level he cares to participate.

The Christian church deserves to die and will indeed die if it does not open itself to the transcendent plan God has for it. This means the total renunciation of war and the rejection of domination and hierarchical structures. It means becoming the servant to the poor and the downtrodden. It means the sacral view of reality and creation, where everything is ultimately to come under the lordship of Christ. It means also the creation of community, where technology and massification do not destroy man's humanity. It means the invitation of every man to join a meaningful community where he belongs and is in communication with his brother.

But Christian man has rejected this vision. He wants the mess of pottage rather than the birthright. Christ looked on Jerusalem and wept, longing for the day when He could take the people under His arms, as a mother hen takes her little ones under her wing. But Christ has not forsaken us, and He has promised that where "two or three are gathered in my name, there I am in the midst." Christ's will can only be done if we everywhere become a band of disciples, in every place a small group, following the Master in intimate fellowship with Him and with the other disciples.

The vision of the free church is the dream of a group of people who will say to their Lord, "Lord, I believe; help thou my unbelief." That the church has never been fully free does not deter us from striving and praying for freedom. The seduction of the environment (Satan) will ever be before us, and we may never become free.

I am not proposing that the discerning and admonishing functions performed in the setting of the small group are the final or only answer. I do not presume to have the solution to the problem of human bondage. I do, however, believe that the small-group structure for discerning God's will is a step in the right direction, and what historical evidence there is seems to corroborate this contention.

EPILOGUE

The free church vision is not unattainable. It is an ideal that is sociologically and theologically possible. Sociologically it is possible along the lines laid down in the argument of the preceding chapters. Theologically it is demanded by what we now know and understand of the dealings of God with His people. The theologies that have emerged which attempt to "degrade" the Christian gospel to the level of "cheap grace," leaving the achievement of the vision of the kingdom of God to an age that is to come, are the saddest examples of ideological thinking.

It has been said that if the churches don't accept the leadership in the areas touched on in this book, they may be thrust into this position even against their wills. If the Christian church doesn't witness to the need for peace, brotherhood, equality, community, and reconciliation, the secular society will literally "put those words in the mouth of the church." And if the church does not assume its responsible role in living the witness, a secular religion will rise up to take its place. A leading sociologist of an earlier generation has stated the case well in the following paragraph:

> We need religion, probably, as much as any age can have needed it. The prevalent confusion, "The tumult of the time disconsolate," is felt in every mind not wholly inert as a greater or less distraction of thought, feeling, and will; and we need to be taught how to live with joy and calm in the presence of inevitable perplexities. A certain natural phlegm is a great advantage in these days, and better still, if we could get it, would be religious assurance. *Never was it more urgent or more difficult to justify the ways of God to men.* . . . There is no prospect that the world will ever satisfy us, and the structure of life is forever incomplete without something to satisfy the need of the spirit for ideas and sentiments that transcend and reconcile all particular aims, whatsoever. . . . Without some regular and common service of the ideal, something in the way of

prayer and worship, pessimism and selfishness are almost sure to encroach upon us. . . . Society is in want of this (religious and social renewal) and the agency that supplies the want will have the power that goes with function — *if not the church, then some secular and perhaps hostile agency*, like socialism, which is already a rival to the church for the allegiance of the religious spirit. [1]

This prophecy of Charles Horton Cooley, said with the authority of an Old Testament prophet, predated the Nazi attempt at a "secular and perhaps hostile agency" by some 25 years.

The secular world is literally forcing the churches into taking their leadership roles. War is probably the best example. For centuries a few persecuted "peace churches" have held on to their conviction that "Peace is the will of God." At the point where the peace churches had almost given up in despair, the societies around the world are beginning to see the light. War is contrary to everything human as is so beautifully couched in the contemporary catchphrase: "War is harmful to children and other living things." The Christian rejection of war is slowly coming to its own, and the tragedy is that the enervated "free churches" are so "shell shocked" that it appears other and more recent converts will pick up the "battle."

But there is more. The concept of brotherhood, the opposite of domination, is being nurtured in many quarters, secular and sacred alike. Business communities are discovering that the concepts of consensus and dialogue are more effective than "tighter organization." Many institutions are beginning to discover that to treat humans as humans pays greater dividends. So again, the secular demands for the rightness of this view are forcing the churches to take their leadership role which they have been allowing to languish.

There is a time for everything, but for many things, that time has passed. There was a time for war, but now the time for peace has come. There was a time to hate, but now the time for love has come. There was a time for refraining from embracing, but now the time for embracing has come. There was a time to rend, but now the time for mending has come. The

Preacher concludes his soliloquy: "I have seen the travail which God hath given to the sons of men to be exercised therewith. He hath made everything beautiful in its time" (Ecclesiastes 3:10).

The march of civilization seems to be heading toward a recognition that the rule of God is the end of life. If the Christian church doesn't lead the march (which I am hopeful it will), a more responsive human movement will. Our Lord, the founder of the Christian church, gave us the mandate when He said, "If ye abide in my word, then are ye truly my disciples; and ye shall know the truth, and the truth shall make you free" (John 8:31, 32).

FOOTNOTES

Chapter 1

1. Anthony F. C. Wallace, *Religion: An Anthropological View* (New York: Random House, 1966), pp. 264, 265.

2. *Ibid.*, p. 258.

3. Kingsley Davis, *Human Society* (New York: Macmillan, 1948), p. 542.

4. Robert Lowie, "Religion in Human Life," *American Anthropologist*, LXV (1963), pp. 533, 534.

5. *Ibid.*, p. 533.

6. Davis, *op. cit.*, p. 509.

7. *Ibid.*, p. 519.

8. Joachim Wach, *Sociology of Religion* (Chicago: The University of Chicago Press, 1944), p. 156.

9. Raoul Narroll, "Does Military Deterrence Deter?" *Transaction*, Vol. 3, January-February, 1966.

10. Kenneth Scott Latourette, *A History of Christianity* (New York: Harper and Brothers, 1953), pp. 408 ff. and 391 ff.

11. *Ibid.*, p. 729

12. George Herbert Mead, *Selected Writings* (Indianapolis: Bobbs-Merrill Co., 1964), p. 360.

13. "War," *Encyclopedia Britannica* (Chicago: Encyclopedia Britannica, 1966), pp. 322-336.

14. Kenneth Boulding, *The Meaning of the Twentieth Century* (New York: Harper and Row, 1964), Colphon ed. 1965 used in this work. Chapter IV, "The War Trap," pp. 75-103.

15. 1 John 3:14, 15, Authorized Version.

16. Amos 5:11, Authorized Version.

17. Hanna H. Meissner, ed., *Poverty in the Affluent Society* (New York: Harper and Row, 1966), p. 46. A detailed list of books on the subject is included. Since her book, numerous other books have appeared on the subject.

18. Luke 4:18.

19. Matthew 25:34 ff.

20. M. C. Gabrielian, *Armenia: A Martyr Nation* (New York: Fleming H. Revell, 1918), p. 92.

21. Norman Cantor, ed., *The Medieval World: 300-1300* (New York: Macmillan Co., 1963), p. 27.

22. Known as Mennonites today, they were originally called Anabaptist, a derogatory manner of referring to their demands that true reform involves rebaptizing the believers.

23. Secularism has been extensively discussed and analyzed. A recent review of the concept can be found in Larry Shiner's "Towards a Theology of Secularization," in *Journal of Religion* (Oct. 1965). See also his "The Concept of Secularization of Values: An Analytical Framework for the Study of Secularization," *The Journal for the Scientific Study of Religion* (Spring, 1969), pp. 112-124.

24. Aldous Huxley, *Time Must Have a Stop* (New York: Harper and Brothers, 1944), p. 131.

25. See Philip M. Hauser, "The Chaotic Society: Product of the Social Morphological Revolution," *American Sociological Review* (Feb. 1969), pp. 1-19.

26. Richard Fagley, *The Population Explosion and Christian Responsibility* (New York: Oxford University Press, 1960).

Chapter 2

1. Robert Nisbet, *The Sociological Tradition* (New York: Basic Books, 1966).
2. *Ibid.*, p. 5.
3. *Ibid.*, pp. 18 ff.
4. *Ibid.*, p.————?
5. *Ibid.*, p. 47.
6. *Ibid.*, p. 56.
7. *Ibid.*, p. 57.
8. *Ibid.*, pp. 84, 85.
9. See, for example, Charles Nordhoff, *The Communistic Societies of the United States* (New York: Harper and Brothers, 1875).
10. Nisbet, *op. cit.*, p. 153.
11. *Ibid.*, p. 151.
12. *Ibid.*, p. 151.
13. *Ibid.*, p. 153.
14. *Ibid.*, p. 156.
15. *Ibid.*, p. 192.
16. *Ibid.*, p. 214.
17. Georg Simmel, *The Sociology of Georg Simmel* (translated by Kurt H. Wolff) (Glencoe: The Free Press, 1950), p. 275. Simmel's treatment of "Super-ordination and Subordination" is a classic statement on the subject.
18. One of the most forceful statements of this problem is H. Richard Niebuhr's *The Social Sources of Denominationalism* (New York: Henry Holt, 1929).
19. Nisbet, *op. cit.*, p. 221.
20. Cf. Robert Bellah, "Religious Evolution," *American Sociological Review*, June 1964, pp. 358-374.
21. Nisbet, *op. cit.*, p. 221.
22. Georg Simmel, "A Contribution to the Sociology of Religion," *American Journal of Sociology*, 1905.
23. Kingsley Davis, *op. cit.*, p. 529.
24. Nisbet, *op. cit.*, p. 264.
25. *Ibid.*, p. 265.
26. *Ibid.*, p. 265.
27. *Ibid.*, p. 266.
28. *Ibid.*, p. 274.
29. Irene Taviss, "Changes in the Form of Alienation: The 1900's vs. the 1950's," *American Sociological Review* (Feb. 1969), pp. 46, 47.
30. Nisbet, pp. 299.
31. *Ibid.*, p. 319.

Chapter 3

1. J. Milton Yinger, *Religion, Society and the Individual* (New York: Macmillan, 1957). See page 266 *passim* for a discussion of the various options delineated here.
2. Christopher Dawson, *Religion and Culture* (New York: Sheed and Ward, 1948), Meridian Book, 1958 edition used in this text, p. 206.
3. Ernst Troeltsch, *Protestantism and Progress* (Boston: Beacon Press, 1958), p. 176.
4. *Ibid.*, pp. 176, 177.
5. *Ibid.*, p. 177.
6. *Ibid.*, p. 176.
7. Soren Kierkegaard, *Attack upon "Christendom"* (Princeton: Princeton University Press, 1944), Beacon paperback, September 1956 edition used in this text, p. 181.

8. "War," *Encyclopedia Britannica,* Volume 23, p. 331 (Chicago: Encyclopedia Britannica, 1966).

9. Roland Bainton, *The Reformation of the Sixteenth Century* (Boston: Beacon Press, 1952), Beacon paperback, 1956 used in this text, p. 155.

10. H. G. Wells, *The Outline of History* (Garden City: Garden City Publishing Company, 1920), p. 672.

11. Louis Brehier, "Crusades," *Catholic Encyclopedia,* Volume IV (New York: Robert Appleton Co., 1908).

12. "Crusades," *Encyclopedia Britannica,* Volume 6, pp. 833, 834.

13. Brehier, "Crusades," *op. cit.,* p. 546.

14. Kenneth M. Setton, *et al., A History of the Crusades* (Philadelphia: University of Pennsylvania Press, 1962), five volumes.

15. "Crusades," *Encyclopedia Britannica,* p. 833.

16. Kenneth M. Setton, *et al.,* Volume II, p. 326.

17. Brehier, "Crusades," *Catholic Encyclopedia,* p. 551.

18. (Garden City, New York: Doubleday and Co., 1961).

19. *Ibid.,* p. 9

20. *Ibid.,* p. 33.

21. Bernard Berelson and Gary A. Steiner, *Human Behavior: An Inventory of Scientific Findings* (New York: Harcourt, Brace and World, 1964), Chapter 17, "Conclusions," p. 659. This proposition has a long and respectable history. Probably the most definitive writer on the subject is Vilfredo Pareto, who says, "At bottom what people want is to think — it matters little whether the thinking is sound or fallacious. . . . This . . . explains the need people feel for covering their non-logical conduct with a varnish of logic — a point we have already stressed time and again and at length" (p. 56) in *Vilfredo Pareto,* ed. by Joseph Lopreato (New York: Thomas Y. Crowell, 1965).

22. Karl Mannheim, *Ideology and Utopia* (New York: Harcourt, Brace and Co., n.d.), p. 55.

23. The following analysis is based upon a wide variety of readings. One heavily used source is T. G. Jalland's *The Origin and Evolution of the Christian Church* (London: Hutchinson's Universal Library, 1948). Other standard church history texts were used, as well as articles in the *Catholic Encyclopedia.* The documentation is deleted since the focus of this discussion is not so much to prove the analysis as to provide the basis for further discussion.

24. Wells, *op. cit.,* p. 555, 556.

25. Kenneth Scott Latourette, *A History of Christianity,* p. 526.

26. *Ibid.,* p. 456.

27. *Ibid.,* p. 414.

28. *Ibid.,* p. 412.

29. *Ibid.,* p. 413.

Chapter 4

1. *The Nation,* March 8, 1958 (p. 199).

2. Leo Tolstoy, "Letter to a Non-Commissioned Officer," in Peter Mayer, ed., *The Pacifist Conscience* (New York: Holt, Rinehart and Winston, 1966), Gateway Ed., p. 164.

3. J. Milton Yinger, *op. cit.,* p. 258.

4. *Ibid.,* p. 237.

5. *Ibid.,* p. 237.

6. Guy F. Hershberger, *War, Peace and Nonresistance* (Scottdale: Mennonite Publishing House, 1953), pp. 374, 375.

7. These are the Friends, Brethren, and the Mennonites. In 1935 these churches adopted a "Plan of Unified Action in Case the United States Is In-

volved in War," though there was cooperation much earlier. See Melvin Gingerich, "Discipleship Expressed in Alternative Service," pp. 262-274, in Guy F. Hershberger, ed., *The Recovery of the Anabaptist Vision* (Scottdale: Herald Press, 1957).

8. Thomas G. Sanders, *Protestant Concepts of Church and State* (New York: Holt, Rinehart and Winston, 1964), p. 81.

9. Peter Rideman, *Account of Our Religion, Doctrine and Faith* (Bungay, Suffolk, England, Hodder and Stoughton, 1950); see also Victor Peters, *All Things Common: The Hutterian Way of Life* (Minneapolis: University of Minnesota Press, 1965) and John A. Hostetler and Gertrude Huntington, *The Hutterites in North America* (New York: Holt-Rinehart-Winston, 1967).

10. Calvin Redekop, *The Old Colony Mennonites: Dilemmas of Ethnic Minority Life* (Baltimore: Johns Hopkins Press, 1969).

11. See *The Way of Love*, January 1966, for a description of their objectives. Little has been written about Reba Place in a comprehensive way.

12. Ernst Troeltsch, *The Social Teaching of the Christian Churches* (New York: Macmillan Co., 1931), Harper Torchbook edition 1960 used in this text, p. 703.

13. Franklin H. Littell, *The Free Church* (Beacon Hill, Boston: Starr King Press, 1957), pp. 62 ff.

14. Franklin H. Littell, *The Anabaptist View of the Church* (American Society of Church History, 1952), p. 32.

15. See Paul Peachey, "The Modern Recovery of the Anabaptist Vision," in Guy F. Hershberger, *op. cit.*, for a trenchant discussion and documentation of this problem.

16. Robert Friedmann, "The Essence of the Anabaptist Faith: An Essay in Interpretation," *Mennonite Quarterly Review*, Volume 41, No. 1, Jan. 1967, p. 24.

17. See Paul Peachey, *op. cit.*, and Franklin H. Littell, "A Working Definition of Anabaptist," in his *The Origins of Sectarian Protestantism* (New York: The Macmillan Co., 1964) for discussions of the way Anabaptism was disparaged as irrelevant. More will be said about this later.

18. Dietrich Bonhoeffer, *The Cost of Discipleship* (New York: Macmillan, 1951), p. 47.

19. John A. Hostetler, *Amish Society* (Baltimore: Johns Hopkins Press, 1963) rev. ed.

20. Calvin Redekop, *op. cit.*, pp. 113-117, "Primary Relationships."

21. J. Milton Yinger, *op. cit.*, p. 250.

22. *Ibid.*, pp. 250, 251.

23. *Ibid.*, pp. 236, 237.

24. Berelson and Steiner, *op. cit.*, pp. 663, 664.

Chapter 5

1. *Christianity and the Social Crisis* (New York: Association Press, 1912), p. 316.

2. *Ibid.*, p. 312.

3. Robert K. Merton, *Social Theory and Social Structure* (Glencoe: The Free Press, 1957), p. 456.

4. *Ibid.*, p. 460.

5. *Ibid.*, p. 470.

6. Karl Mannheim, *op. cit.*, p. 9.

7. Franklin H. Littell, *The Origins of Sectarian Protestantism, op. cit.*, pp. 206, 207 footnote.

8. Thomas G. Sanders, *op. cit.*, p. 80.

9. *Ibid.*, p. 80.

10. *Ibid.*, p. 81.

11. Rauschenbusch, *op. cit.*, p. 401.

12. Latourette, *op. cit.*, pp. 785, 786.

13. Mannheim, p. 13.

14. *Ibid.*, p. 211.

15. *Ibid.*, p. 3.

16. *Ibid.*, p. 46.

17. John S. Oyer, "Reformers Oppose the Anabaptists," in Guy F. Hershberger, ed., *The Recovery of the Anabaptist Vision, op. cit.*, pp. 206 ff.

18. John Horsch, *Mennonites in Europe* (Scottdale: Mennonite Publishing House, 1950), p. 34.

19. *Ibid.*, p. 34, 35.

20. Mannheim, pp. 39, 40.

21. *Ibid.*, p. 57.

22. Horsch, *op. cit.*, p. 35.

23. *Ibid.*, p. 41, 42.

24. *Ibid.*, p. 41.

25. *Ibid.*, p. 40.

26. Mannheim, p. 34.

27. Milton M. Gordon, *Assimilation in American Life* (New York: Oxford University Press, 1964), p. 29.

28. See Michael Novack, "The Free Churches and the Roman Church," *Journal of Ecumenical Studies*, Fall, 1965, pp. 426-447.

29. See Paul Peachey, *Die soziale Herkunft der Schweizer Taüfer in der Reformationszeit* (Karlsruhe: Buchdruckerei und Verlag Heinrich Schneider, 1954).

30. Oyer, p. 210.

31. Franklin H. Littell, "The Anabaptist Concept of the Church," in Guy F. Hershberger, *The Recovery of . . .* , p. 123.

32. *Ibid.*, p. 126.

33. *Ibid.*, p. 127.

34. See Emile Durkheim, *The Elementary Forms of the Religious Life* (London: George Allen and Unwin, 1915).

35. Fritz Blanke, "Anabaptism and the Reformation," in Guy F. Hershberger, *The Recovery of . . .* , pp. 59 ff.

36. John Horsch, *Mennonites in Europe* (Scottdale: Mennonite Publishing House, 1950), p. 194.

37. This idea was first elaborated by Richard Myers, a student in a course in "Theories of Social Organization." It is not possible to make a definitive case for this proposition, namely, that the Anabaptists were the first to stress the concept of "group charisma." Harold S. Bender, for example, presumes to establish as "fact" that Conrad Grebel was the leader of the Swiss Anabaptists. See his "Conrad Grebel, the First Leader of the Swiss Brethren" (Anabaptists), *MQR*, Volume X, Number 1, January 1936. However, a careful reading of his own argument based on data he cites can be interpreted the opposite way. It is much easier to establish that Anabaptism emerged on the basis of "group charisma" than to prove that there were not other groups that emerged the same way and hence might either support or refute the present thesis.

38. John C. Wenger, "The Biblicism of the Anabaptists," in Guy F. Hershberger, *The Recovery of . . .* , p. 168.

39. *Ibid.*, p. 169.

40. John A. Hostetler, *Anabaptist Conception of Childrearing and Schooling* (Philadelphia: Temple University, 1968), mimeographed, p. 69.

Chapter 6

1. Though a vast amount of information is already available, foremost scholars believe that great amounts must still be done before an adequate picture will emerge. A series of research organizations are now sponsoring such research and projecting more. See the *Mennonite Life* (North Newton: Bethel College) annual report entitled "Mennonite Research in Progress," esp. the July 1968 issue, for descriptions of the major organizations sponsoring research.

2. Sanders, *op. cit.*, pp. 94, 95.

3. Robert Kreider, *Mennonite Quarterly Review*, Volume 25, Number 1, January 1951, p. 18, 22.

4. *Ibid.*, p. 33.

5. Harold S. Bender, "The Anabaptist Vision," in Guy F. Hershberger, *op. cit.*, p. 54.

6. Robert Friedmann, *op. cit.*, p. 10.

7. Bainton, *op. cit.*, p. 96.

8. *Ibid.*, p. 97.

9. Friedmann, p. 24.

10. *Ibid.*, p. 9.

11. Bender, *op. cit.*, p. 52.

12. *Ibid.*, p. 52.

13. See Wolfgang Schäufele, *Das missionarische Bewusstsein und Wirken der Täufer: dargestellt nach oberdeutschen Quellen* (Neukirchen: Neukirchen Verlag des Erziehungsvereins, 1966).

14. Quoted in Guy F. Hershberger, *The Recovery of . . .* , p. 163.

15. *Bainton, The Reformation*, p. 98.

16. Numerous typologies of Anabaptism have been present, the most notable being Harold S. Bender's three points in his "The Anabaptist Vision" (discipleship, concept of the church, and love and nonresistance).

17. "Anabaptism and the Reformation," in Guy F. Hershberger, *The Recovery of . . .* , p. 60.

18. *Ibid.*, pp. 60, 61.

19. J. Lawrence Burkholder, "The Anabaptist Vision in Discipleship," in Guy F. Hershberger, *The Recovery of . . .* , p. 137.

20. John Howard Yoder, "Binding and Loosing" (Pamphlet Series, No. 14), February 1967. The entire issue is devoted to the concept of congregational discipline and edification, and contains a classic statement by Balthasar Hubmaier. The subject is most comprehensively treated by Marlin Jeschke, "Toward an Evangelical Conception of Corrective Church Discipline" (unpublished PhD dissertation, Field of Religion, Northwestern University, 1965).

21. Ernst Troeltsch, *The Social Teachings of the Christian Churches* (New York: Macmillan Co., 1931), Harper Torchbook edition used in this text, pp. 695 ff.

22. *Christ and Culture* (New York: Harper and Brothers 1951), Harper Torchbook edition used in this volume.

23. E. Clinton Gardner, *The Church as a Prophetic Community* (Philadelphia: Westminster, 1967), p. 183.

24. *Ibid.*, p. 186.

25. *Ibid.*, p. 189.

26. J. W. Stevenson, *God in My Unbelief* (London: Collins, 1960), p. 151.

Chapter 7

1. See Donald F. Durnbaugh, "Theories of Free Church Origins," *Menno-*

nite Quarterly Review (April 1968), Volume XLI, Number 2, for a brief treatment of the theories of free churches. See also Ernst Troeltsch who says, "The essential meaning of the free church system, on the contrary, is the destruction of the medieval and early Protestant idea of a social order welded together by one uniform State Church, and of one infallible authority with a uniform control of the whole of civilization." *The Social Teachings . . .* , p. 656.

2. See Ernst Troeltsch, *ibid.,* pp. 656 ff.; see also Franklin H. Littell, "Voluntarvism," in his *The Free Church,* p. 61.

3. *Ibid.,* "The Free Church vs. Totalitarianism," pp. 90-112.

4. *Ibid.,* "The Free Church and Its Discipline," pp. 113-131; see esp. John Howard Yoder, "Binding and Loosing," *Concern,* No. 14 (Scottdale, Feb. 1967). For a penetrating discussion of this point, see Marlin Jeschke, *op. cit.,* p. 22, where he makes the significant statement that the Christian church's (both Protestant and Catholic) lack of concern about church discipline (admonition and restoration) appears to be evidence that the church chose to overlook those doctrines which it did not want to enforce! This is probably the most powerful argument of the self-deception of the Christian church.

5. See a typical sociology of religion textbook such as Thomas Ford Hoult, *The Sociology of Religion* (New York: Dryden Press, 1958), which has a chapter entitled "The Stratification Order and Religion."

6. John H. Redekop, *The American Far Right: A Case Study of Billy James Hargis and Christian Crusade* (Grand Rapids: Eerdmans, 1967).

7. The concept of the "divine order" cannot be definitively treated here. This concept has Quaker origins, beginning with Robert Barclay and continuing in Lewis Benson. See Lewis Benson. "The Order that Belongs to the Gospel," *Concern,* July, 1959 pp. 41-55

8. The concept of subjectivity is as old as human thought. Plato wrote about the shadows of the cave (The Republic, Book VII) and about the fact that man would rather stay in a dark cave than confront the light of the sun.

9. For an earlier version of this outline, see Calvin Redekop, *The Church Functions with Purpose* (Scottdale: Mennonite Publishing House, 1967).

10. Latourette, *op. cit.,* p. 667.

11. *Layman's Bible Commentary* (Richmond: John Knox Press, 1959) p. 29.

Chapter 8

1. The documentation for the interaction theory presented here will not be presented. Many of the concepts used here are in a sense arbitrary, depending upon the user's purposes. Hence, the designation small could as well use the figure 20 or 30, rather than 25. But there is a general limit. The same goes for other concepts used. For a general introduction to small group theory, see Michael S. Olmsted, *The Small Group* (New York: Random House, 1959).

2. A. Paul Hare, Edgar F. Borgatta, and Robert F. Bales, *Small Groups: Studies in Social Interaction* (New York: Alfred A. Knopf, 1965). This conforms to a profile developed by Hare but does not presume to be representative.

3. James 2:24, Phillips.

4. Horst Symanowski, *The Christian Witness in an Industrial Society* (Philadelphia: Westminster, 1964).

Epilogue

1. Charles Horton Cooley, *Social Organization* (New York: Charles Scribner's Sons, 1909), Free Press Reprint, 1956 used in this book, p. 376 *passim.*

INDEX

182

Doukhobors, 24

Dualism, Anabaptist, 108

Durkheim, Emile, 34; and authority, 36; and sacred, 41; cited, 100

Dutch Mennonites, decline of, 106

Dutch Reformed Church in Africa, 24

Economic conditions limited by, 88

Economic processes, 116

Edification, in community, 109

Edifices, religious, 12

Education, in church, 125

Emigration: of Mennonites, 72; only recourse, 113

Enclaves, of Old Colony, 113

Enlightenment, 26

Environment: conditioned by, 50; goals of, 123

Epistemology, group nature of, 103

Equality: of sects, 71; and church, 171

Eschatology, implications for, 121

Established church: Catholic Church as, 113; within Old Colony system, 114

Ethnic group, Anabaptists as, 97

Ethnocentrism: concept, 75; principle, 84

Ethical urge, of Anabaptists, 108

Excommunication and ban: in Mennonite Church, 111; in Old Colony, 113; Anabaptist stress on, 141

Excommunication, as domination, 23

Exploitation: social and economic, 21; of masses, 93; in Old Colony, 117

Faith: confessional, 5; faith in, 84; common care of, 101

Faithfulness, expression of, 66

Fallacy of misplaced concretion: defined, 50; discussed, 120

Fallibility, aware of, 125

False consciousness, tragic, 48

Family, as Gemeinschaft, 33

Fatalism, of lower class, 40

Feedback: from bishops, 60; in groups, 153; and preaching, 157

Fellowship: spiritual, 7; in sect, 71; of believers, 124

Feudal system, as Gemeinschaft, 34

Folk ceremony, 139

Fourth of July: and religion, 168; as rationalization, 168

Free, in truth, 173

Freedom, communal, 8

Free church: concept, 123, 125; emerge, 128; as tradition, 8; defined, 71; essence of, 83; awareness of, 84; concept, 86; vision, 106, 121; and Christ-culture dimension, 120

Freedom, preservation of, 123

Folk church, 119

Friedmann, Robert, quoted, 107

Frustrations, of young, 8

Function, of individual, 159

Functions: of religion, 15, 43; of small group, 154-156; of discerning and sanctioning, 156

Functionalism, and religion, 42

Gathered church: expression of, 97; concept of, 99

Gemeinschaft: transition from, 28; defined, 32; relation to Gesellschaft, 33; of Mennonite community, 79; of world, 130

Germantown, 75

Gesellschaft, transition to, 28; defined, 32; in city, 33; relationship to Gemeinschaft, 33; world, 130

Gifts: delineated, 159; applied, 160

God: will of, 3, 72, 123; scientific, 25; particular, 84; rule of, 173

Gospel: as total ideology, 59; unfaithful to, 95; of love, 18

Great Commission, discipleship as, 110

Grebel, Conrad: quoted, 95; as leader, 100, 101

Group nature, of Anabaptism, 99; of theology, 100

Hamarskjöld, Dag, 83

Hargis, Billy James, 125

Hierarchies, as concept, 38

Historic peace churches, 72

Historical relativities, rejection of, 111

Holy City: Franks ejected, 55; free, 66

Holy Sepulchre: pilgrimmages to, 52; free the, 66

Holy Roman Empire, and Catholic Church, 61

Holy Spirit, key issue, 127

Horsch, John, quoted, 109

Hostility: caused by secularism, 27; toward Catholic Church, 112; among Old Colony, 117

Human condition, nature of, 86

Human institution, philosophy of, 88

Human relations: variations in, 129; framework of, 129; length of, 129; depth of, 129; breadth of, 129

Hussites, 141

Hutter, Jacob, 73

Hutterites: and domination, 24; sharing in, 73; and technology, 79

Hypocrisy, in holy office, 93

Identification, with group, 98

Identity, universal, 82

Ideology: particular, 57; defined, 57; German, 58; total, 58; of capitalism, 58; particular, 100

Ideology, total: victim of, 68, 94; possibility of, 68; of author, 71; protest, 88; perceive, 92; issue of, 93

Idolatry, of Jews, 51

Incarnation, of gospel, 47

Inclusion-exclusion, and small group, 162

Indignation of Anabaptists, 93

Individualism: concern with, 37; increasing, 43; total, 44; Western, 126

Industrial society, secondary nature of, 131

Institution, church as, 108

Integration: of church, 61; into economic life, 63

Integrity, individual's, 43

Intellect, development of, 26

Intellectual tradition, revolution in, 89

Interaction: random, 152; units of, 152; amount, 153

Interpretation, of Anabaptists, 98

Intimacy: human, 8; in human relations, 129

Ireland, conflict in, 50

Islam, triumph of, 52

Isolation of Old Colony, 113

Israel, fallacy of, 51

Jehovah's Witnesses, and coercion, 24

Jesus: critical of Judaism, 16; quoted, 50

Jerusalem: capture of, 52; Christ wept over, 169

Judaism: and criticism, 15; Jesus and, 16; and monotheism, 25

K groups: functions of, 166; rules of thumb, 166; frequency of meetings, 167; size of, 167

Kierkegaard, Soren: cited, 16; quoted, 49

Kingdom: inherit, 20; earthly, 118

Kingdom of God: ideal of, 5; church as, 73; and state, 76; live in, 77; life in, 78; in Scriptures, 78; image of, 82; higher cause of, 83; member of, 84; true, 95; loyalty to, 95; attempted here, 107; as behavior, 108; missionaries for, 109; promoting, 110; concept of, 111

Kinship, as *Gemeinschaft*, 32

Koinonia group: strategy of, 128; as peer group, 142; help to Christians, 143; Christian, 144

Knowledge: for what, 68; accumulated, 135

Kreider, Robert, quoted, 106

Laity/clergy, in sect, 71

Large gathering: function of 147-150; forms of, 147-151; limitations of, 149; individual in, 149

Latourette, Kenneth Scott, cited, 62

Lazarus: teaching on, 19; listen to, 169

Leader, charismatic, 101

Leaders: Anabaptist, 98; installed by people, 101; charismatic, 101

Leadership and church, 171

Life, disciplined, 7

Littell, Franklin, quoted, 99

Lord: confession of, 141; mandate of, 173

Lordship of Christ, rejected by Christendom, 120

Lowie, Robert, cited, 14

Loyalty, universal, 82

Loyalties, other, 83

Luther, Martin, support of princes, 125

Lutherans, in World War II, 65

Mannheim, Karl: cited, 57; quoted, 89

Marx, Karl: views of, 38; an aliena-

authenticity of, 144; concept, 144; and canon, 145

Perceptions: conditioned, 84; exceptional, 98; personalized, 158

Perceptual grid, establishing, 134

Perfectability, implications for, 121

Persecution: of peace churches, 72; of Jews, 140

Perspectives, analytical, 66

Pharisees, as ideology, 59

Phillips, Dirk, 101

Philosophy, of every age, 88

Piety: acts of, 66; symbolic expressions of, 66; individual, 108

Pluralism: introduced, 91; incipient, 92

Pluralistic thought, emergence of, 89

Polarization, radical, 8

Policeman, in society, 161

Politicians: circumvention of, 139; and laws, 140

Poor, and Christianity, 19

Pope Urban, and Crusades, 52

Population: world, 14; density, 27; among Mennonites, 79; pressure, 80; and technology, 80

Potential, of Christian church, 47

Poverty: extent of, 19; glorification of, 20; life of, 20

Power: and authority, 35; and sect, 80; rejection of, 94; political, 118

Priests, activities of, 61

Priesthood of all believers, defined, 138

Primary type relations, Christian and, 131

Principle, tacit, 50

Primary group: fosters discernment, 137; defined, 138; witness as to needs, 130

Prisoner, Christian, 127

Professionals, in church, 137

Progress, in evolution, 65

Proletariat, and ideology, 58

Prophets: of Judaism, 15, 19; Old Testament, 172

Property, of church, 61, 62

Protestant, Christian, 48

Protestantism, in modern world, 49

Protestant Christian, committed, 48

Proximity, in small groups, 161

Prussia, migration to, 72

Public life, of small group, 161

Public morality, 126

Puritan Church, 22

Quakers: and slavery, 75; as *Ketzer*, 80

Rational method, 120

Rationalization, self, 126

Rauschenbusch, Walter: quoted, 88, 91

Reality: apprehended, 57; external, 57; false, 58; objective, 59; pervert, 85

Reciprocity principle, 85

Reconciliation, and church, 171

Reformation: radical, 7; wars of, 17; origin of Anabaptists, 72; missionaries in, 75; coming accelerated, 92; and state, 93

Reformation leaders, equivocation of, 93

Reformed Church, in Africa, 140

Relationship, deepening of, 161

Relevance: of Christian faith, 119; concept of, 119

Relief and service, concern for, 74

Religion: civil, 5, 6, 7; American, 5; Christian, 47; primitive, 37; departments of, 15; fate of, 12; social, 68

Religions: revivals of, 12; shape of, 13; world, 14, 15; universal, 71

Religious movement, authentic, 8

Religious practice, Christian, 168

Renaissance, coming accelerated, 92

Renewal, in congregation, 167

Resentment, of exploitation, 93

Revivals, evangelical, 7

Revolution, scientific, 26

Rich, and Christianity, 19

Ridemann, Peter, 73

Role identity, confused, 136

Role segregation, in society, 136

Roman Catholic Church: and secularism, 26; and population, 28

Roman Empire, and Christian church, 24

Rural life, of Mennonites, 78

Russia, migration to, 72

Sacraments, 110

Sacred, concept of, 40
Salvation, implications for, 121
Sanitation, relation to health, 27
Sanders, Thomas G., cited, 90
Schisms, in Mennonite Church, 111
Scholars, Anabaptists as, 99
Schwärmer, Anabaptists as, 99
Science, advance of, 12
Scriptures: teach, 3; reading of, 92; only followed, 93; whole, 102; source, 103
Secularism: an environment, 25; and Christianity, 25; as value-free, 26; measures of, 26; importance to church, 27; and Mennonites, 77
Secular age, protest of, 80
Sect: defined, 114; "church against the world," 119
Sect groups: unseduced, 70; eschatology of, 83; rank of, 125
Sect-type groups, 118
Seduction: of Crusades, 63; secular, 123; reason for, 134
Self-deceit: congregational, 127; denominational, 127; recognized, 128
Self-deceiving principle, 85
Self-delusion, free from, 106
Seljukian Turks, and domination, 21
Semi-communal, Old Colony Mennonites, 73
Separation: of church and state, 5, 81; of free church, 83; from world, 109, 113
Separated life, Old Colony, 113
Sermon on the Mount, 56; mutual concern of, 75
Sign of cross, marching under, 66
Simmel, Georg, 40, 42
Simons, Menno, quoted, 102
Sin: free from, 123; aware of, 123
Slavery, first statement, 75
Small groups: strengths of, 155; ministries of, 155; key in discernment, 158; introducing in congregation, 163; and members, 165
Social conditions, determined, 88
Social environment, variety in, 130
Social relations: dimensions of, 128; segmental nature of, 136
Social situation, break with, 95

Social structure: and population, 28; of discernment, 147; value of, 147
Social worship, in large gathering, 149
Society: religion in, 14; sacred, 25; mass, 28
Sociologists, and sacred, 41; Christian, 31; nonreligious, 70; American, 124
Sociology, and religion, 15
Sociology of knowledge, defined, 89
Solidarity: social, 34; ecclesiastical, 50
Spain, Catholic Church in, 81
Spirit, of age, 70
Spirit of God, decides, 93
State: Mennonite rejection of, 74; separation from, 83; and church, 96; nonparticipation in, 113; Old Colony as, 115
Status: rejected, 101; in small group, 159
Status quo, Zwingli and, 83
Status systems, justification of, 40
Stratification, and sect, 80
Strong/weak, in sect, 71
Structure of accountability: principle of, 141; method of, 142
Structure for discernment, in primary group, 134, 138
Structural support: in army, 134; of promise, 140
Structure: hierarchial, 60; bureacratic, 60; of church, 63
Struggle, religious, 8
Subjectivism, involved in, 126
Subjectivity, of human behavior, 88
Success, of war, 65
Suffering, of Crusades, 55
Sunday school, God's will for, 136
Supernaturalism, fate of, 12
Survival: reproduction for, 27; of church, 161
Sutton, K. M., 53
Swiss Brethren, confession of, 102
Switzerland, Zwinglian church in, 81
Subconscious, theory of Freud, 57
Symanowski, Horst, 158
Symbol: of piety, 66; more consistent, 67

187

Teaching, in large gathering, 149

Technology: advance of, 12; avoided by Mennonites, 79; changing, 28; level of, 27

Temporal order, relation of Christ to, 118

Testimony, to government, 72

Theologian, setting of, 135

Theological apparatus, warped, 127

Theologizing, group nature, 101

Theology: as religion, 16; and sociologists, 62; of Christian church, 62

Thirty Years' War: account, 49; Bainton on, 50

Thought: determined, 88; patterns of, 89; modes of, 89; processes, 89; group source of, 92; roots of, 93, 94; motivations of, 94; community source of, 100; social source, 102

Titans, of sociology, 42

Tocqueville, Alexis de, and authority, 36, 44

Tönnies, Ferdinand, 32; cited, 33

Total ideology: concept of, 95; free from, 95; refused, 96; protest, 98; realize, 102; victim of, 106

Tradition: and small groups, 162, 163; of theologians, 135; Mennonite, 80; radical, 7

Transcendental dimension, of secularism, 25

Transcendental nature, of church, 48

Troeltsch, Ernst, 48, 49, 50, 74, 99, 114

Truth: know the, 173; related to times, 135

Turks: persecution by, 52; ejected Franks, 55

Two-kingdom ethic, of Mennonites, 77

Unconscious victim, of environment, 64

Unit ideas, five, 31

Units: of interaction, 152, 153; of input, 152

Unified society, breakup of, 92

Unitary world view: breakdown, 92; rejection of, 93

Universalism, in religion, 71

Unsound eyes, all have, 57

Urbanization, among Mennonites, 79

Values, of society, 124

Value systems, of congregation, 168

van Leiden, Jan, 101

Vision: is a dream, 170; attainable, 171; of kingdom of God, 171

Vladimir, of Russia, 17

Voice, of God, 83

Volkskirche: and Anabaptists, 90; rejection of, 90, 91; rebaptizing of, 91; Russian Mennonites as, 107; membership in, 115, 124; Lutheran Church as, 119

Voluntary pledge, 139

Voluntary religion, 117

Vows, faithfulness to, 140

Wach, Joachim, cited, 16

Waldensians, sect, 80

Wallace, Anthony, cited, 12

War: and Christianity, 17; statistics on, 17; as trap, 18; as environment, 18; is harmful, 172

Warfare: history of, 17; rejected, 72

Watershed, in history, 89

Way of the cross, rather than war, 72

Wealth: stance toward, 20; Christ and, 20; skeptical, 73; amassing, 127

Wealthy/poor, in sect, 71

Weber, Max: on class, 39; cited, 45

Wells, H. G., 51

Weltanschauung, 63; particular, 96

Wesley, John, 141

West, and religion, 15

Wiedertaufer, referred to, 99

Will, natural, 32

Williams, George, cited, 7

Winter, Gibson, cited, 56

Word: divine, 95; claims of, 96

Words, of proclamation, 158

World, Old Colony became the, 117

World War II: and national churches, 25; horror of, 58

World view, of Anabaptists, 96

"Worldly people," "mixing with," 116

Yinger, J. Milton, quoted, 70, 81, 82

Young, frustrations of, 8

Zeal, missionary, 97

Zwingli: conflict with, 83; felt secure, 94; rejected, 95; view of, 98

Zwinglian leaders, relation to state, 93

Calvin Redekop was born in 1925 of parents who homesteaded on the newly opened Fort Peck Indian Reservation in Montana. He took his BA at Goshen College, his MA at the University of Minnesota, and his PhD at the University of Chicago. His major training is in social theory, sociology of religion, and the sociology of minorities. He also studied a year at Goshen College Biblical Seminary.

He has been a college and seminary teacher since 1954, having taught at Hesston College, Hesston, Kansas; Tabor College, Hillsboro, Kansas; Earlham College and Earlham School of Religion, Richmond, Indiana; Goshen College and the Associated Mennonite Biblical Seminaries, Goshen, Indiana.

His writings include numerous articles in church periodicals, several booklets in the Herald Press Focal Pamphlet Series, a book entitled *The Old Colony Mennonites: Dilemmas of Ethnic Minority Life* (Johns Hopkins Press, 1969), and numerous articles in professional journals.

He spent three years in relief work in Europe after World War II, working especially with young people. He conducted work camps in most European countries. He is an active layman, a member of several denominational committees, and presently serves as an elder of the Goshen College Mennonite Church, Goshen, Indiana. He has a wife, Freda, and three boys. He is currently doing research on, and writing about, communal societies, and the Armenians.